Que® Quick Reference Series

Excel® Quick Reference

Hy Bender

Que® Corporation
Carmel, Indiana

This book is based on Microsoft Excel: IBM Version 2.1 and the earlier Version 2.0.

Que Quick Reference Series

The *Que Quick Reference Series* is a portable resource of essential microcomputer knowledge. Whether you are a new or experienced user, you can rely on the high-quality information contained in these convenient guides.

Drawing on the experience of many of Que's best-selling authors, the *Que Quick Reference Series* helps you easily access important program information.

Now it's easy to look up often-used commands and functions for 1-2-3, dBASE IV, WordPerfect 5, Microsoft Word 5, and MS-DOS, as well as programming information for C, Turbo Pascal, and QuickBASIC 4.

Use the *Que Quick Reference Series* as a compact alternative to confusing and complicated traditional documentation.

The *Que Quick Reference Series* includes these titles:

1-2-3 Quick Reference
1-2-3 Release 2.2 Quick Reference
1-2-3 Release 3 Quick Reference
Assembly Language Quick Reference
AutoCAD Quick Reference
C Quick Reference
dBASE IV Quick Reference
DOS and BIOS Functions Quick Reference
Excel Quick Reference
Hard Disk Quick Reference
Harvard Graphics Quick Reference
MS-DOS Quick Reference
Microsoft Word 5 Quick Reference
Norton Utilities Quick Reference
PC Tools Quick Reference
QuickBASIC Quick Reference
Turbo Pascal Quick Reference
WordPerfect Quick Reference

Publishing Director
Lloyd J. Short

Product Director
Karen A. Bluestein

Developmental Editor
Shelley O'Hara

Editor
Cheryl Robinson

Technical Editor
Ron Holmes

Indexer
Sharon Hilgenberg

Production
Corinne Harmon
Jennifer Matthews
Bruce D. Steed

Table of Contents

Introduction

Excel Quick Reference is not a rehash of traditional documentation. Instead, this quick reference is a compilation of the most frequently used information from Que's best-selling Microsoft Excel books.

Excel Quick Reference presents essential information on Excel commands, functions, and macros for Excel. You will learn the proper use of primary Excel functions, as well as how to avoid serious errors. This book contains fundamental information in a compact, easy-to-use format, but is not intended as a replacement for the comprehensive information presented in a full-size guide. You should supplement this quick reference with one of Que's complete Excel texts, such as *Excel Quickstart, Using Excel: IBM Version,* or *Excel Tips, Tricks and Traps.*

Excel Quick Reference is divided into sections. The Command Reference is an alphabetical listing of all Excel commands. Each command is presented in the same format. The *Purpose* briefly explains what the command does, the *Procedures* provide steps you follow to use the command, and *Notes* provide comments, tips, or suggestions for using the command.

Following the Command Reference are sections on Worksheet Functions, Macro Functions, and Macro Key Codes.

Now you can put essential information at your fingertips with *Microsoft Excel Quick Reference*—and the entire Que Quick Reference Series!

AN EXCEL OVERVIEW

You can use Microsoft Excel to perform repetitive math calculations, analyze data, and draw graphs and charts.

Use Excel commands for functions such as copying or moving portions of the worksheet, formatting cells to display currency, and using the database. You access Excel commands through a variety of menus.

Choosing Menu Items

The *menu bar*, the second line in the worksheet window, shows the current menu selections. You can choose a menu item using the keyboard or the mouse.

To choose a menu item using the keyboard:

1. Press **Alt** to activate the menu bar.

2. Press the underlined letter in the menu you want to see. (It does not matter whether you type the letter in upper- or lowercase.) In this book, the keys you press are blue.

   Dimmed commands are not available for selection.

To choose a menu item using the mouse:

1. Move the pointer to the name of the menu you want.

2. Click to see the menu.

3. Move the pointer to the option you want.

   Dimmed commands are not available for selection.

4. Click to select an option.

If the command name ends in an ellipsis (), a dialog box appears prompting you for more information. In most cases the command executes immediately.

Using Dialog Boxes

Dialog boxes can consist of up to five of the following elements:

> A *List box* is a rectangular area that displays a list of choices .

> A *Text box* is a rectangular area in which you can type relevant text or numbers.

> A *Check box* is a small, square box used to turn on or off a particular option.

> An *Option button* is a small, round button used to turn on one of a group of options.

> A *Command button* is a large, rounded rectangle labeled with a particular action.

Using the keyboard, you can move around a dialog box by pressing **Tab** to go forward and **Shift+Tab** to go backward.

To select a dialog box option, press and hold **Alt** and press the underlined letter or number in the option. If you are using a mouse, move to the option and click.

Pressing the **space bar** or selecting the default command button turns an active checkbox on or off. Pressing **Enter** also selects the active command button because this button often contains the command OK. Pressing **Enter** is usually the fastest way of accepting the dialog settings, closing the dialog box, and executing the menu command. Pressing **Esc** always selects the Cancel command button, which usually cancels your dialog settings and then closes the dialog box.

Navigating

To move to a cell using the mouse, move the pointer to the cell you want and click. If the cell is not on-screen, first use the scroll bars until the cell appears.

Use the **Num Lock** key to toggle between pointer movement and 10-key entry.

The following keystrokes also move the cursor while Excel is in EDIT mode. A plus sign between keys indicates that you press the keys at the same time.

Key(s)	Function
←	Moves cell pointer one cell left.
→	Moves cell pointer one cell right.
↑	Moves cell pointer up one cell.
↓	Moves cell pointer down a cell.
Home	Moves cell pointer to the beginning of the current row.
End	Moves cell pointer to the end of the current row.
Home	When Scroll Lock is on, moves the cell pointer to the start of the window.
End	When Scroll Lock is on, moves the cell pointer to the end of the window.
PgUp	Moves cell pointer up a screen.
PgDn	Moves cell pointer down a screen.
Ctrl+PgUp	Moves cell pointer one screen left.
Ctrl+PgDn	Moves cell pointer one screen right.
Ctrl+Home	Moves cell pointer to cell A1.
Ctrl+End	Moves cell pointer to last cell.
Ctrl+←	Moves cell pointer left to the next intersection of a blank cell and a cell that contains data.

Ctrl+→	Moves cell pointer right to the next intersection of a blank cell and a cell that contains data.
Ctrl+↑	Moves cell pointer up to the next intersection of a blank cell and a cell that contains data.
Ctrl+↓	Moves cell pointer down to the next intersection of a blank cell and a cell that contains data.
F5 (GoTo)	Prompts for a cell reference, range, or range name. After you enter the information and press Enter, the cell pointer moves directly to and selects the requested reference.
Alt,W,*window#*	Moves cell pointer from the current (active) window to another window whose number you specify.

Selecting Objects

Some commands require that you select a cell, range, multiple area, chart object, or other item. To unselect something, select anything else (for instance, move to a cell without pressing Shift).

Use the following keystrokes to select while Excel is in EDIT mode:

Key(s)	*Function*
Shift+	Selects as you move. Combine Shift with any of the movement keys listed in the preceding section.
Shift+space bar	Selects an entire row.
Ctrl+space bar	Selects an entire column.

Shift+Ctrl+ space bar	Selects the entire worksheet.
F8 (Extend)	Puts Excel in Extend mode, extending the selection as you move (as if you kept **Shift** pressed). To end Extend mode, press **F8** again.
F5 (GoTo)	Prompts for a cell reference, range, or range name. After you enter the information and press **Enter**, the cell pointer moves directly to and selects the requested reference.
F8, F5	Extends a selection from the current (active) cell to the cell you move to using **F5**.

Moving Within a Selection

The usual cursor-movement keys cause a selection to collapse. To move within a selection, use the following keys:

Key(s)	*Function*
Tab	Moves the cell pointer one cell to the right.
Shift+Tab	Moves cell pointer one cell to the left.
Enter	Moves cell pointer down one cell.
Shift+Enter	Moves cell pointer up one cell.
Ctrl+Tab	Moves cell pointer to the next selected range.
Shift+Ctrl+Tab	Moves cell pointer to the preceding selected range.

Using Function Keys

Function keys save time when you edit cells, move between windows, save files, and get help. Your keyboard contains 10 or 12 function keys, labeled F1 through F10 or F1 through F12, respectively. Excel supports all 12 keys, but Alt+F1 duplicates all F11 functions, and Alt+F2 duplicates all F12 functions.

Following is a list of all function keys and function key combinations, and the command equivalents:

Key(s)	Command
F1	Help
Shift+F1	Context-sensitive Help
Alt+F1	File New (Chart)
Alt+Shift+F1	File New (Worksheet)
Alt+Ctrl+F1	File New (Macro sheet)
F2	Edit formula in formula bar
Shift+F2	FoRmula Note
Ctrl+F2	Window Show Info
Alt+F2	File Save AS
Alt+Shift+F2	File Save
Alt+Ctrl+F2	File Open
Alt+Ctrl+Shift+F2	File Print
F3	FoRmula Paste Name
Shift+F3	FoRmula PasTe Function
Ctrl+F3	FoRmula Define Name
Ctrl+Shift+F3	FoRmula Create Names
F4	FoRmula Reference
Ctrl+F4	Control Close (document window)
Alt+F4	Control Close (application window)
F5	FoRmula Goto
Shift+F5	FoRmula Find (cell contents)
Ctrl+F5	Control Restore (document window)

COMMAND REFERENCE

The command reference is an alphabetical listing of all Microsoft Excel commands. Each command appears in the same format: the command name is boxed, followed by the keys you press to select the command. When a command is available only under certain conditions, those conditions are noted in parentheses.

Chart Add Arrow

Alt, C, R (chart)

Purpose

Adds an arrow to a chart. Use repeatedly to add multiple arrows of various sizes, colors, weights, and styles.

Procedures

To add an arrow:

1. Press **Alt, C, R** or click the **C**hart menu and select Add A**R**row.

2. Move the arrow to the location you want using the Forma**T** Mo**V**e command or the mouse.

3. Resize the arrow with the Forma**T** Si**Z**e command or with the mouse.

4. Format the arrow using the Forma**T** **P**atterns command.

To delete an arrow:

1. Select the arrow.

2. Select **C**hart Delete A**R**row.

Chart Add Legend

Alt, C, L (chart)

Purpose

Adds a legend to a chart so that you can identify the different objects in the chart.

Procedures

To add a legend:

1. Press Alt, C, L or click the Chart menu and select Add Legend.

   The legend appears on the right side of the chart.

2. Select the legend and choose the FormaT Legend command to reposition the legend.

3. Select the legend and choose the FormaT Patterns and FormaT Font commands to format the legend.

To delete a legend:

Select the Chart Delete Legend command. Added legends assume the formatting of the deleted legend.

Notes

The plot area resizes to make room for added legends.

The Patterns and Font commands are available through the Format Legend dialog box, as well as through the FormaT menu.

Chart Add Overlay

Alt, C, O (full menus) (chart)

Purpose

Overlays a second chart over the current (main) chart to create combination charts. The data series is evenly divided between the main chart and overlay chart. If an odd number of data exists, the main chart gets the extra data series (for example, if you have five data series).

Procedures

To add an overlay:

1. Press **Alt**, **C**, **O** or click the **C**hart menu and select Add **O**verlay.

2. Change the overlay's chart type and format by selecting the Forma**T** **O**verlay command.

To delete the overlay:

Select the **C**hart Delete **O**verlay command.

Chart Attach Text

Alt, C, T (chart)

Purpose

Inserts text near a chart object, such as the title, the axes, or a data series. If you move or resize a chart object, the text moves or resizes along with it.

Procedures

To attach text:

1. Select the chart object to which you want the text attached.

2. Press **Alt**, **C**, **T** or click the **C**hart menu and select Attach **T**ext.

3. Select Chart **T**itle, **V**alue Axis, **C**ategory Axis, or Series or **D**ata Point.

4. Press **Enter** or click OK.

5. Type the text you want in the formula bar and press **Enter**.

6. Select Forma**T** **T**ext to format the text.

To revise attached text:

1. Select the text. The text appears in the formula bar.

2. Edit the text.

Chart Axes

Alt, C, X (chart)

Purpose

Displays or hides the category and value axes.

Procedures

1. Press **Alt**, **C**, **X** or click the **C**hart menu and select the Chart A**X**es command.

2. From the dialog box, select the axes you want to hide or display.

3. Press **Enter** or click OK.

Note

When an axis is hidden, the plot area resizes to fill the extra space.

Chart Calculate Now

Alt, C, N, or F9 (chart)

Purpose

When manual calculation is on, recalculates all open worksheets, and then redraws all open charts supported by those worksheets.

Procedures

Press **Alt**, **C**, **N** or **F9** or click the **C**hart menu and select Calculate **N**ow.

Note

For this command to have an effect, the worksheets supporting the charts must be open.

Chart Delete Arrow

Alt, C, R (chart)

Purpose

Deletes a selected arrow from a chart.

Procedures

1. Select the arrow.

2. Press Alt, C, R or click the Chart menu and select Delete ARrow.

Chart Delete Legend

Alt, C, L

Purpose

Deletes the legend from a chart.

Procedure

Press Alt, C, L or click the Chart menu and select Delete Legend. The plot area resizes to fill the extra space.

Chart Delete Overlay

Alt, C, O (full menus) (chart)

Purpose

Deletes the overlay chart, making the main chart incorporate the data series.

Procedure

Press Alt, C, O or click the Chart menu and select Delete Overlay.

Chart Full Menus

Alt, C, M (short menus) (chart)

Purpose

Sets all menus to display all options.

Procedure

Press **Alt**, **C**, **M** or click the **C**hart menu and select Full **M**enus.

Chart Gridlines

Alt, C, G (chart)

Purpose

Displays or hides major and minor gridlines attached to the category and value axes.

Procedures

1. Press **Alt**, **C**, **G** or click the **C**hart menu and select the **G**ridlines command.

2. Set Category Axis **M**ajor Gridlines, Category Axis M**I**nor Gridlines, Value Axis Maj**O**r Gridlines, and/or Value Axis Mi**N**or Gridlines.

3. Press **Enter** or click OK.

The gridlines display or hide as you specify.

Chart Protect Document

Alt, C, P (full menus) (chart)

Purpose

Safeguards a chart's data series, formats and window from change. Optionally provides password protection.

Procedures

1. Press **Alt**, **C**, **P** or click the **C**hart menu and select the **P**rotect Document command.

2. Optionally turn on **C**ontents to protect the chart's current data series and formats.

3. Optionally turn on **W**indows to protect the chart's window screen position, size, and other characteristics.

4. Select **P**assword and enter a password consisting of up to 16 letters, numbers, and symbols.

5. Press **Enter** or click OK. The specified aspects of the chart lock.

Note

An ideal password is simple for you to remember, but hard for others to guess. You cannot make changes to the chart's settings unless you have the password.

Chart Select Chart

Alt, C, C (chart)

Purpose

Selects all elements of a chart, enabling Forma**T** setting changes and **E**dit commands to affect all aspects of the chart.

Procedures

1. Press **Alt**, **C**, **C** or click the **C**hart menu and choose Select **C**hart.

2. Use the Forma**T** commands to alter the chart elements.

3. Use the **E**dit Cl**E**ar command to delete the chart's data series or formats.

4. Use the **E**dit **C**opy command to copy the chart's data series or formats to another chart.

To unselect the chart, press an arrow key or click the mouse.

Chart Select Plot Area

Alt, C, A (chart)

Purpose

Selects a chart's plot area, enabling FormaT Patterns setting changes to affect all elements in the area bounded by the axes.

Procedures

1. Press Alt, C, A or click the Chart menu and select Plot Area.

2. Optionally use the FormaT Patterns command to change the border style, border color, border weight, background pattern, background color, or foreground color of the area bounded by the axes.

   Unselect the chart by pressing an arrow key or clicking the mouse.

Chart Short Menus

Alt, C, M (full menus)

Purpose

Sets all menus to display only the most-used options to make Excel simpler for beginners learning the program.

Procedure

Press Alt, C, M or click the Chart menu and select Full Menus.

Chart Unprotect Document

Alt, C, P (full menus)

Purpose

Removes safeguards created by the Chart Protect Document command.

Procedures

1. Press Alt, C, P or click the Chart menu and select the UnProtect Document command.

   If you do not password protect the chart, you can alter it. If you password protect the chart, you must supply the password to alter the chart.

2. Type the appropriate password and press Enter or click OK, if necessary.

If you do not enter the correct password, Excel beeps and displays an error message, keeping the chart protected. Repeat Step 2, this time supplying the appropriate password.

Control Close

Alt, space bar, C, or Alt+F4
Alt, -, C, or Ctrl+F4

Purpose

Closes the active application or document window.

Procedures

To close an application window:

Press Alt, space bar, C or Alt+F4 or click the Application Control menu and select Close.

To close a document window:

Press Alt, -, C or Ctrl+F4 or click the Document Control menu and select Close.

Control Maximize

Alt, space bar, X, or Alt+F10
Alt, -, X, or Ctrl+F10

Purpose

Expands the active window to fill the screen space.

Procedures

To expand an application window:

Press **Alt**, **space bar**, **X** or **Alt+F10** or click the Application Control menu and select Ma**X**imize.

To expand a document window:

Press **Alt**, **-**, **X** or **Ctrl+F10** or click the Document Control menu and select Ma**X**imize.

Notes

In document windows you maximize, the Control menu dash that normally appears at the document's top left corner changes to a slightly smaller dash to the left of the menu.

Control **R**estore returns a window to its preceding size and location.

Control Minimize

Alt, space bar, N, or Alt+F9

Purpose

Provides more on-screen space by collapsing the application window to a small icon at the bottom of the screen.

Procedures

Press **Alt**, **space bar**, **N** or **Alt+F9** or click the Application Control menu and select Mi**N**imize.

To restore the window to its preceding size and location, press **Alt**, **space bar**, **R** or **Alt+F5**.

Control Move

Alt, space bar, M, or Alt+F7
Alt, -, M, or Ctrl+F7

Purpose

Moves the active window.

Procedures

To move an application window:

1. Press **Alt**, **space bar**, **M** or **Alt+F7** or click the Application Control menu and select **M**ove.

2. Press the arrow keys to move the window in the direction you want. Press and hold **Ctrl** while pressing the arrow keys to move in smaller increments.

3. After positioning the window, press **Enter**.

To move a document window:

1. Press **Alt**, **-**, **M** or **Ctrl+F7** or click the Document Control menu and select **M**ove.

2. Press the arrow keys to move the windowt. Press and hold **Ctrl** while pressing the arrow keys to move in smaller increments.

3. After you position the window, press **Enter**.

If you are using a mouse, drag a window by dragging the window's title bar.

Control Restore

Alt, space bar, R, or Alt+F5
Alt, -, R, or Ctrl+F5

Purpose

Restores a window to its preceding size and location. This command does not affect changes made by the Control **S**ize and Control **M**ove commands.

Procedures

To restore an application window:

Press **Alt**, **space bar**, **R** or **Alt+F5** or click the
Application Control menu and select **R**estore.

To restore a document window:

Press **Alt**, **-**, **R** or **Ctrl+F5** or click the Document
Control menu and select **R**estore.

═ Control Run ═══════════════════

Alt, space bar, U

Purpose

Runs the **C**lipboard, the Control **P**anel, the **M**acro
Translator, or the **D**ialog Editor.

Procedures

1. Press **Alt**, **space bar**, **U** or click the Application
   Control menu and select R**U**n.

2. Select the **C**lipboard to see the contents, the Control
   Panel to adjust system settings, the **M**acro
   Translator to convert Lotus 1-2-3 macros to Excel
   macros, or the **D**ialog Editor to create custom
   dialog boxes.

3. Press **Enter** or click OK.

═ Control Size ═══════════════════

Alt, space bar, S, or Alt+F8
Alt, -, S, or Ctrl+F8

Purpose

Changes the size of the active window.

Procedures

To change the size of an application window:

1. Press **Alt**, **space bar**, **S** or **Alt+F8** or click the Application Control menu and select **S**ize.

2. Press the arrow keys to resize the window. To resize the window in smaller increments, press **Ctrl** and the appropriate arrow key.

3. When the window is the size you want, press **Enter**.

To change the size of a document window:

1. Press **Alt**, **-**, **S** or **Ctrl+F8** or click the Document Control menu and select **S**ize.

2. Press the arrow keys to resize the window. To resize the window in smaller increments, press **Ctrl** and the appropriate arrow key.

3. When the window is the size you want, press **Enter**.

If you are using a mouse, resize a window by dragging its gray border.

Control Split

Alt, -, T

Purpose

Divides the active document window into two linked panes that scroll together.

Procedures

1. Press **Alt**, **-**, **T** or click the Document Control menu and select Spli**T**.

2. Press the arrow keys to move the split panes pointer until you have the desired division.

3. Press **Enter**.

If using a mouse, you can drag the split bars from the solid black rectangles that appear near the window's bottom left and top right corners.

Note

This command is available for worksheets and macro sheets only.

Data Delete

Alt, D, D (full menus)

Purpose

Erases database records that match the criteria in the criteria range, and causes subsequent records to move up to fill the empty space. This command has no effect on worksheet data outside the database.

Procedures

1. Define your database range and criteria range using the Data Set DataBase and Data Set Criteria commands.

2. Enter your criteria.

3. Optionally, preview the data you want to delete using the Data Find or Data Extract command.

4. Press Alt, D, D or click the Data menu and select Delete.

Note

Because you cannot undo the effects of the Data Delete command, be careful of what you specify for elimination. Do not include blank rows in the criteria range, as this matches and deletes all records in the database.

Data Exit Find

Alt, D, F

Purpose

Exits the Find mode initiated by the Data Find command.

Procedure

When you finish examining matched records in Find mode, press **Alt**, **D**, **D** or click the **D**ata menu and select Exit **F**ind. The scroll bars return to normal.

Data Extract

Alt, D, E (full menus)

Purpose

Copies database records that match specified criteria into the extract range.

Procedures

1. Define your database range and criteria range using the **D**ata Set Data**B**ase and **D**ata Set **C**riteria commands.

2. Enter your criteria.

3. Select the range of cells you want to hold the extracted data. The first row of the range should contain the names of the database fields you want to work with.

   If you select the first row and rows below it, the extracted data copies to those rows only, erasing preceding data. Excel copies as much data as it can and then displays an error message.

   If you select the first row alone, all following rows define as part of the extract range, eliminating extract space limitations. However, the rows clear, whether data copies to them or not.

4. Press **Alt**, **D**, **E** or click the **D**ata menu and select the **E**xtract command.

5. Optionally select to extract **U**nique Records Only. This filters out duplicate database records.

6. Press **Enter** or click OK. The records matching your criteria copy to the extract range.

Notes

Only the formula's value extracts from records containing formulas.

Because you cannot reverse this clearing with Edit Undo, use this option with care.

Data Find

Alt, D, F

Purpose

Selects records in the database that match your criteria in the criteria range.

Procedures

1. Define your database range and criteria range using the Data Set DataBase Data and Set Criteria commands.

2. Set your criteria.

3. Press Alt, D, F, or click the Data menu and select Find.

   If the active cell is outside the database when you execute the command, the first record that matches the criteria is selected. If the active cell was in the database, the record following the active cell that matches the criteria selects. Also, the scroll bars become striped to show you are in Find mode.

4. Move across fields in the selected record by pressing Tab or Enter to go right, Shift+Tab or Shift+Enter to go left.

5. Move to the next or preceding matching record by pressing the down- or up-arrow key, or clicking the down or up scroll box. Excel beeps when it finds no more matches.

6. Move to the next or preceding matching record at least a page away by pressing PgDn or PgUp or by clicking below or above the scroll bar. When there are no more matches, Excel beeps.

7. Scroll the screen up to the length of the database by pressing the right- or left-arrow keys or by dragging the scroll box.

8. When you finish examining the matched records, press Esc, select the Data Exit Find command, or click a cell outside the database. The scroll bars return to normal.

Notes

One of these operators must precede criteria: =, >, <, >=, <=, or <>.

To perform a backward search, press Shift as you select Find.

Data Form

Alt, D, O

Purpose

Enables you to view, find, edit, add, and delete database records, thus offering an alternative to many of the Data menu commands.

Procedures

To access the database form:

1. Define your database range using the Data Set DataBase command.

2. Press Alt, D, O, or click the Data menu and select the FOrm command.

   The left side of the dialog box contains a list of all database field names. To the right of each field is its entry for the first record.

3. To move among entries, use the following keys:

Key	Action
Tab	Moves among current record entries.
Shift+Tab	Moves among current record entries.

Enter	Moves to the top of the next record.
Shift+Enter	Moves to the top of the preceding record.
Ctrl+PgUp	Moves to the first record.
Ctrl+PgDn	Moves to the last record.
Down-arrow	Moves to the same field in the next record.
Up-arrow	Moves to the same field in the preceding record.

The upper right of the screen shows your record number and how many records are in the database, and the scroll bar in the center visually indicates your location in the database.

To add new records:

1. Access the database form.

2. Select NeW, or click and drag the center scroll box to the bottom of the database form. You move to an empty record at the bottom of the database.

3. Enter new data in the fields you want.

4. Save the data and move to the next empty record by pressing Enter.

5. Select EXit.

To remove a record:

1. Access the database form.

2. Move to the record.

3. Select Delete and press Enter or click OK. The record deletes, and Excel renumbers all subsequent records.

4. Select EXit.

To change a field entry:

1. Access the database form.

2. Move to and edit the database field.

3. Select EXit.

To find specific records:

1. Access the database form.

2. Select Criteria to display criteria options.

3. Select Clear to remove preceding entries.

4. Enter criteria for the appropriate field(s). (This criteria is totally separate from the criteria range, which Data FOrm ignores.)

5. Select Find Next to display the next matching record or Find Prev to find the preceding matching record.

6. Select EXit.

Data Parse

Alt, D, P (full menus)

Purpose

Distributes imported records across multiple columns.

Procedures

1. Select cells within a column that each contain multiple records (typically the result of importing data from another application).

2. Press Alt, D, P, or click the Data menu and select the Parse command.

   The records in the first cell of your range appear on the Parse Line.

3. Select Clear to clear brackets indicating where the data should be split up into separate records.

4. Select Guess to make Excel insert brackets in the spots it guesses for splitting the data.

5. Edit the Parse Line by inserting and deleting brackets where appropriate.

6. Press Enter or click OK. Selected cells are parsed based on the bracket placements in the first cell.

Data Series

Alt, D, R (full menus)

Purpose

Fills selected range with a series of numbers based on the value in the first cell and your command settings.

Procedures

1. Enter the starting values in the first row or first column of your range.

2. Select the range.

3. Press **Alt, D, R**, or click the **D**ata menu and select the Se**R**ies command.

4. Select to fill the range based on the starting values in its **R**ows or **C**olumns.

5. Enter the **S**tep Value, which is the amount by which each successive cell in the range increases.

6. Select **L**inear to add the **S**tep Value to each successive cell, **G**rowth to multiply the **S**tep Value by each successive cell, or **D**ate to generate a series of numeric dates.

7. If you select **D**ate, also select whether you want to progress the dates by D**A**y, **W**eekday, **M**onth, or **Y**ear.

8. Optionally, enter a St**O**p Value to set a number-generation ceiling, unless you want numbers generated to the end of the range.

9. Press **Enter** or click OK.

Data Set Criteria

Alt, D, C

Purpose

Defines the range of cells containing the database criteria.

Procedures

1. Select a range of cells you want to hold the database criteria. Placing the criteria range above the database, keeps the criteria in sight.

   The range must be at least two rows. The first row contains the names of the database fields you want to work with, and the following rows contain the criteria.

2. Press Alt, D, C, or click the Data menu and select Set Criteria. Excel defines the database, and names the range Criteria.

Notes

You must precede criteria with one of the following operators: =, >, <, >=, <=, or <>.

You can define only one criteria range at a time in a worksheet. However, you can set up multiple ranges in the criteria format and then use this command to quickly reassign the criteria definition to any of the ranges.

Refer to criteria in other worksheets by using the FoRmula Define Name command to insert the name of the other worksheet and an exclamation point in front of the criteria name.

Data Set Database

Alt, D, B

Purpose

Defines the range of cells comprising the database.

Procedures

1. Select a range of cells to hold the database. The cells can be blank or contain data.

   The range must be at least three rows. The first row must contain the field names, the following rows the database records and a blank row.

2. Press **Alt, D, B**, or click the **D**ata menu and select Set Data**B**ase. Excel defines the database, and names the range Database.

Notes

Put the database just below the criteria range to keep the criteria in sight and within ready reach.

A database can be as large as the entire worksheet (that is, 256 fields and 16,383 records), but it is not necessary to select all rows when defining. As long as your range includes a totally blank last row, the database automatically redefines as it grows.

You can define only one database at a time in a worksheet. However, you can set up multiple ranges in the database format and then use this command to quickly reassign the database definition to any of the ranges.

You also can refer to databases in other worksheets by using the For**M**ula **D**efine Name command to insert the name of the other worksheet and an exclamation point in front of the Database name.

Data Sort

Alt, D, S

Purpose

Orders selected records based on a key row or column.

Procedures

1. Define your database range using the **D**ata Set Data**B**ase command.

2. Select the records in the database to sort. (Do not include the field names.)

3. Press **Alt, D, S**, or click the **D**ata menu and select the **S**ort command.

4. Choose to sort by **R**ows or by **C**olumns.

5. Enter the **1**st Key sort. If you select **R**ows in Step 4, specify a column by which you want to sort. If you

select Columns in Step 4, specify a row by which you want to sort.

6. Choose whether you want to sort by Ascending or Descending order.

7. Optionally enter other sort keys, and repeat Steps 5 and 6.

8. Press Enter or click OK.

Data Table

Alt, D, T (full menus)

Purpose

Repeatedly substitutes a value in a specified cell with values from a selected range, then generates a "what if" table based on the values resulting from a specified formula or formulas.

Procedures

To create a single-input table:

1. In a single row or single column, create a list of substitute values for a particular cell.

2. Directly to the left of the row or above the column, enter a formula whose results vary with each substitute value. (Optionally enter additional formulas directly below or to the right of the first formula.) Each formula should refer to the cell into which the list of values, one by one, substitutes.

3. Select your list(s) and formula(s).

4. Press Alt, D, T, or click the Data menu and select Table.

5. Enter the cell reference which you want your list of values substituted. If your list is in a row, enter the reference in the Row Input Cell box. If it's in a column, enter the reference in the Column Input Cell box.

6. Press Enter or click OK. A list of "what if" results generates.

To create a two-input table:

1. In a row and a column directly to the left of the row, create two lists of substitute values for two particular cells.

2. In the upper left corner of the list, enter a formula whose results vary with each pair of substitute values by referring to both cells in which the lists of values substitutes.

3. Select your list(s) and formula(s).

4. Press **Alt, D, T,** or click the **D**ata menu and select **T**able.

5. Enter the cell references in which you want your lists of values substituted. For the list in the row, enter the reference in the **R**ow Input Cell box. For the list in the column, enter the reference in the **C**olumn Input Cell box.

6. Press **Enter** or click OK. A list of "what if" results generates.

Edit Clear

Alt, E, E or Del

Purpose

Removes data, formats, and notes from charts and worksheets. Removes selected characters from the formula bar.

Procedures

1. Activate the formula bar and select part or all of the formula.

2. Press **Alt, E, E,** or **Del,** or click the **E**dit menu and select Cl**E**ar.

3. If a dialog box appears, select from the button that describes what you want to clear from **A**ll , Forma**T**s, Fo**R**mulas, or **N**otes. Then press **Enter** or click OK.

For charts, select **A**ll, Forma**T**s, or Fo**R**mulas,

meaning the data series. Then press **Enter** or click OK.

Notes

Do not confuse this command with **E**dit **D**elete, which removes not only a cell's contents and formatting but the cell itself.

A cleared cell has a value of zero in formulas.

Edit Copy

Alt, E, C or Ctrl+Ins

Purpose

Copies a range of cells, characters from the formula bar, or an entire chart to another location.

Procedures

1. Select a rectangular range of cells, characters from the formula bar, or an entire chart.

2. Press **Alt**, **E**, **C** or **Ctrl+Ins**, or click the **E**dit menu and select **C**opy.

   A marquee appears around your selection, and the data and formatting of your selection copies to the Clipboard.

3. Go to where you want to insert a copy.

4. To make only one copy, press **Enter**.

   To make multiple copies, use the **E**dit **P**aste or **E**dit Paste **S**pecial commands. Then press **Esc**.

Notes

This command has no effect on the original range.

If you press **Shift** as you select the **E**dit menu, the **C**opy Picture command replaces this command.

Excel also provides the following "quick copy" alternatives:

Ctrl+'	Copies the contents of the active cell to the preceding cell.
Ctrl+"	Copies the contents of the preceding cell to the active cell.
Ctrl+Enter	Copies data entered in the formula bar to a range of selected cells, filling the range.

See also Edit Fill DoWn, Edit Fill Left, Edit Fill RigHt, and Edit Fill Up commands.

Edit Copy Picture

Alt, Shift+E, C (shifted command)

Purpose

Copies a pictorial representation of selections to the Clipboard for use in another application.

Procedures

1. Select the range you want to copy (the selection restrictions on Edit Copy do not apply here).

2. Press Alt, Shift+E, C, or press Shift, click the Edit menu and select the Copy Picture command.

3. In a worksheet or macro sheet, select whether you want the picture's appearance As Shown on Screen or As Shown when Printed. In a chart, additionally select the same options for the picture's size.

4. Press Enter or click OK.

   A picture of your selection copies to the Clipboard.

5. Go to where you want to insert the picture, and use the other application's Paste command to insert the range.

Notes

The original selection is not affected by this command.

This command is useful when you create reports that mix text and graphics.

Edit Cut

Alt, E, T or Shift+Del

Purpose

Moves data and formatting to another location.

Procedures

1. In a worksheet or macro sheet, select a rectangular range of cells or select characters from the formula bar. In a chart, select characters from the formula bar.

2. Press Alt, E, T, or Shift+Del or click the Edit menu and select CuT.

3. If you select a range of cells, go where you want to move the range's data and formatting, and press Enter.

   If you select characters from the formula bar, the characters appear in the Clipboard. Go where you want to move the characters, and select the Edit Paste command. The characters appear where you indicate. A copy of the characters remains in the Clipboard, enabling you to make multiple copies.

Notes

Do not confuse this command with Edit Delete or Edit ClEar, which remove data, as opposed to move data.

In a chart, you can cut objects or characters only from the formula bar.

Edit Delete

Alt, E, D or Ctrl+- (dash)

Purpose

Removes specified cells (and all associated data and formatting) from the worksheet, shifting surrounding cells into their place.

Procedures

1. Select the cell(s) you want to remove.

2. Press **Alt**, **E**, **D**, or **Ctrl+-** or click the **E**dit menu and select **D**elete.

   If you select entire columns or rows in Step 1, surrounding columns or rows shift to fill the deleted cells. Otherwise, Excel prompts you to choose Shift Cells **L**eft or Shift Cells **U**p.

3. If you do not select the cells, choose either Shift Cells **L**eft and Shift Cells **U**p and press **Enter** or click OK.

Notes

Formulas that refer to the deleted cells cannot locate the cells and display the error value #REF!.

See also **E**dit Cl**E**ar, which removes a cell's data, formatting and notes, but leaves the cell in place.

Edit Fill Down

Alt, E, W or Ctrl+< (left angle bracket)

Purpose

Copies the data and formats of the top of a range down through the rest of the range.

Procedures

1. Select one or more ranges.

2. Press **Alt**, **E**, **W** or **Ctrl+<** or click the **E**dit menu and select Fill Do**W**n.

The data and formats of the top of your ranges copy into the selected cells below them. The ranges remain selected for further commands.

Notes

Copied data replaces existing cell contents.

See also **E**dit **C**opy.

Edit Fill Left

Alt, Shift+E, H (shifted command)

Purpose

Copies the data and formats of the right column into the rest of the range.

Procedures

1. Select one or more ranges.

2. Press Alt, Shift+E, H, or press Shift, click the Edit menu, and select Fill Left.

The data and formats of the right column of your ranges copy into the selected cells to the left. The ranges remain selected for further commands.

Notes

This command has no effect on the right column of the range you copy.

See also Edit Copy.

Edit Fill Right

Alt, E, H or Ctrl+> (right angle bracket)

Purpose

Copies the data and formats of the left column of a range into the rest of the range.

Procedures

1. Select one or more ranges.

2. Press Alt, E, H or Ctrl+>; or click the Edit menu and select Fill RigHt.

The data and formats of the left column of your ranges copy to the selected cells to the right. The ranges remain selected for further commands.

Notes

This command has no effect on the left column of the range you copy, but Excel erases the destination cells.

See also Edit Copy.

Edit Fill Up

Alt, Shift+E, W (shifted command)

Purpose

Copies the data and formats of the bottom of a range to the rest of the range.

Procedures

1. Select one or more ranges.

2. Press Alt, Shift+E, W or press Shift, click the Edit menu and select Fill Up (W).

The data and formats of the bottom of the range copy to the selected cells. Ranges remain selected for further commands.

Notes

This command has no effect on the range you are copying, but does erase the the destination cells.

See also Edit Copy.

Edit Insert

Alt, E, I or Ctrl-+ (plus sign)

Purpose

Inserts a blank cell or range, pushing existing cells to the right or down. Formulas that refer to the moved cells are revised to correspond to the new location.

Procedures

1. Select a range the size of the cells you want to insert.

2. Press **Alt**, **E**, **I** or **Ctrl-+** or click the **E**dit menu and select the **I**nsert command.

   If you select entire columns or rows in Step 1, Excel inserts the columns or rows, causing surrounding columns or rows to shift respectively. If you do not select entire columns or rows, choose Shift Cells **R**ight or Shift Cells **D**own.

3. If you do not select a range, select Shift Cells **R**ight or Shift Cells **D**own. Then press **Enter** or click OK.

Edit Paste

Alt, E, P or Shift+Ins

Purpose

Pastes a copy of the Clipboard's contents in a specific location. Preceded by Excel's **E**dit commands or a comparable command from another application.

Procedures

1. Examine the Clipboard with the Control **RU**n command, making sure that the Clipboard contains the information you want. Use **E**dit **C**opy or **E**dit Cu**T** from within Excel, or a comparable command from another application to insert information in the Clipboard.

2. Go to where you want to insert a copy, and press **Alt**, **E**, **P** or **Shift+Ins** or click the **E**dit menu and select **P**aste.

The copy appears in the new location. Using **E**dit **C**opy, or **E**dit Cu**T** enables you to continue pasting, making multiple copies in multiple locations.

Note

This command is often the easiest way to transfer data between documents and across applications.

Edit Paste Link

Alt, E, L (full menus)

Purpose

Pastes formula(s) with absolute references referring to a cell or range copied to the Clipboard. A change in the original mirrors in its copies. Generally preceded by the Edit Copy command, or a comparable command from another application.

Procedures

1. Make sure that the Clipboard contains the information you want to paste. Use Edit Copy from within Excel, or a comparable command from another application to insert the information.

2. Go to where you want to insert a linked copy.

3. Press Alt, E, L or click the Edit menu and select Paste Link.

Excel inserts the absolute reference formula(s). In most cases you can continue pasting, making multiple copies in multiple locations.

Note

You also can paste link from another application. If more than one cell copies, the command pastes an array.

Edit Paste Special

Alt, E, S (full menus)

Purpose

Pastes specified portions of the Clipboard's contents in a specific location. Preceded by the Edit Copy command or a comparable command from another application.

Procedures

1. Examine the Clipboard with the Control RUn command, making sure the Clipboard contains the

information you want. Use the Edit Copy command or a comparable command from another application to insert information in the Clipboard.

2. Go to where you want to insert a copy

3. Press Alt, E, S or click the Edit menu and select Paste Special.

4. A dialog box appears offering the following pasting options: All, FoRmulas, Values, FormaTs, or Notes.

5. If you choose All, FoRmulas or Values, select how you want to combine the copied data with the destination cells. The options are NOne, which replaces the paste area data with the copied data; ADd, which adds the copied data to the paste area data; Subtract, which subtracts the copied data from the paste area data; Multiply, which multiplies the copied data and the paste area data; and DIvide, which divides the paste area data by the copied data.

6. Turn on Skip Blanks to skip copying blank cells from the Clipboard.

7. Turn on TransposE to switch the orientation of the copied data.

8. Press Enter or click OK.

Precede this command with Edit Copy to continue pasting, making multiple copies in multiple locations.

Notes

Use this command to format new worksheets with a variety of cell properties you create for an existing worksheet.

Use this command to convert formulas to values by copying, selecting the Values option, and then pasting the copies over the originals.

Edit Repeat

Alt, E, R or Alt+Enter (full menus)

Purpose

Repeats certain Excel operations.

Procedures

1. Perform an Excel operation that Repeat can do (for example, apply a format to a cell, then move to another cell to repeat applying the format).

2. Press Alt, E, R, or Alt+Enter or click the Edit menu and select Repeat.

The operation can repeat until you do another operation.

Note

The message `Can't Repeat` appears on the Edit menu if the operation cannot replay.

Edit Undo

Alt, E, U or Alt+Backspace

Purpose

Reverses many Excel operations, including entering or editing worksheet data, all Edit commands, FoRmula Apply Names, FoRmula REplace, FormaT Justify, Data Parse, and Data Sort commands. Can undo the most recent operation only.

Procedures

1. Perform an Excel operation that Undo can reverse.

2. Press Alt, E, U or Alt+Backspace, or click the Edit menu and select Undo. The document appears the way it was before the operation.

   If you want the document as it was after the operation, immediately select Redo (U), which

replaces Undo on the Edit menu. To return to the
preoperation worksheet, immediately select Undo.

Note

Undo provides a powerful safety net, and enhances the
"what if" exercises in the worksheet.

File Close

Alt, F, C

Purpose

Closes the active document and its window(s).

Procedures

1. Press Alt, F, C or click the File menu and select
   Close.

   If the document has unsaved changes, Excel asks
   whether you want to save the file.

2. If the document has unsaved changes, select Yes to
   save the document and close the window(s). Select
   No to abandon your changes and close the
   window(s). Select Cancel (by pressing Esc or
   clicking the option) if you do not want to save the
   file and close the window. When you select Cancel,
   you return to the document as if you did not select
   the command.

Notes

Make sure that you save your document before closing
unless you are certain you do not need the latest
changes.

If you have multiple windows and just want to close an
extra window, select the Control Close command.

To close all documents, select the File Close All shifted
command.

File Close All

Alt, Shift+F, C (shifted command)

Purpose

Closes all open documents and their windows.

Procedures

1. Press Alt, Shift+F, C or press Shift, or click the File menu and select Close All.

   If a document has unsaved changes, Excel asks whether you want to save the file.

2. If you have unsaved changes, select Yes to save the document. Excel asks about the next document.

   Select No, and Excel asks about the next document. Excel eventually asks about every open document with unsaved changes. It then closes all documents and their windows. Documents for which you selected No lose their latest changes.

If you select Cancel at any point, no files close, and you return to the active document. However, the files you save before you selected Cancel remain saved.

Notes

Make sure that you save documents before closing to avoid loss of changes.

File EXit triggers the File Close All command.

File Delete

Alt, F, D (full menus)

Purpose

Permanently deletes a file from disk.

Procedures

1. Press Alt, F, D or click the File menu and select the Delete command.

Files in the current directory appear in the Files box.

2. Select from or type the file in the Files box.

3. Press **Enter** or click OK and press **Enter** or click Yes.

Note

Scroll through the file list using the down and up arrow keys, **PgDn** and **PgUp**, or the scroll bar.

Available drives and directories appear in the Directories box. To display files in different ways, use DOS DIR options in the File Name box.

You cannot retrieve deleted files.

File Exit

Alt, F, X

Purpose

Closes open documents, their windows, and exits Excel.

Procedures

1. Press **Alt, F, X** or click the **F**ile menu and select E**X**it.

   If a document has unsaved changes, Excel asks whether you want to save the file.

2. If Excel prompts you to save files, select **Y**es to save the document or **N**o. Excel asks about every open document with unsaved changes and then closes all documents and their windows, saves the Clipboard, and exits to the operating system. Documents for which you select No lose the latest changes.

   If, instead, you select Cancel (by pressing **Esc** or clicking the option) at any point, the entire operation is canceled. You remain in Excel, no files close, and you return to the active document. However, the files you save before you select Cancel remain saved.

Note

To close all windows but remain in Excel, select the File
Close All command.

File Links

Alt, F, L (full menus)

Purpose

Lists the supporting documents of the active linked
document and enables you to open any supporting
documents. You also can switch links to a different
document.

Procedures

To open linked documents:

1. Activate the linked document you want to work
   with.

2. Press Alt, F, L or click the File menu and select
   the Links command.

   The names of all linked documents appear in the
   Links box. Scroll through the list using the arrow
   keys, PgDn and PgUp keys, or the scroll bar.

4. Select the file or files you want to open. To
   select adjoining files, press Shift+up- or down-
   arrow keys. To select non-adjoining files, press
   Ctrl+up or down arrow to move through the list
   and the space bar to select the files.

5. Turn on the Read Only option when you want
   only to see and not change the files.

6. To open your selected file(s), press Enter or
   click Open.

To switch a link to a different document:

1. Activate the linked document you want to work
   with.

2. Press **Alt**, **F**, **L** or click the **F**ile menu and select the **L**inks command.

3. Select the supporting document you want to change and then select **C**hange. A second dialog box appears.

4. Select from or type the name in the **F**iles box, and press **Enter** or click OK.

File New

Alt, F, N

Purpose

Creates a new worksheet, chart, or macro sheet in a new window. The number of open documents is limited only by your system's memory.

Procedures

1. Press **Alt**, **F**, **N**, or click the **F**ile menu and select **N**ew.

   Excel asks whether you want to create a **W**orksheet, **C**hart, or **M**acro Sheet.

2. Select the type of document you want to create and press **Enter** or click OK.

The document appears in a new window, and you are placed in the document. A new worksheet or macro sheet is blank and assumes the settings of the **O**ptions **W**orkspace dialog box. A new chart is blank unless you select worksheet data, which plots the data.

Note

Pressing **Alt+Shift+F1** or **Shift+F11** opens a new worksheet, **Alt+F1** or **F11** opens a new chart, and **Alt+Ctrl+F1** or **Ctrl+F11** opens a new macro sheet.

File Open

Alt, F, O or Alt+Ctrl+F2 or Ctrl+F12

Purpose

Opens an existing file so that you can work with it.

Procedures

1. Press Alt, F, O; Alt+Ctrl+F2, or Ctrl+F12 or click the File menu and select the Open command.

   Files in the current directory appear in the Files box.

2. Select the file from the Files box or type its name in the File Name box.

3. Press Enter or click OK. Press Enter or click Yes to confirm your choice. The file opens.

Notes

Scroll through the file list using the down- and up-arrow keys, PgDn, PgUp, or the scroll bar.

Available drives and directories appear in the Directories box. Select the drive and directory you want and press Enter or click OK, and those files appear in the Files box.

To display files in different ways (such as with drive prefixes and wildcards), use DOS DIR options in the File Name box.

Turn on the Read Only option when you want only to see and not change the files. (This option is applicable to networks, where several people may use the same file simultaneously.)

This command also can open a file that re-creates your previous workspace by opening and positioning all documents you were using when you saved the workspace.

In addition to its own Normal format, Excel can open files in the following formats:

> Text   Also called ASCII, a generic PC format.

CSV	Comma Separated Values.
SYLK	Used by other Microsoft worksheets.
WKS	Used by Lotus 1-2-3 Release 1A..
WK1	Used by Lotus 1-2-3 Release 2.
DIF	Data Interchange Format.
DBF 2	Used by dBASE II.
DBF 3	Used by dBASE III and dBASE III Plus

File Page Setup

Alt, F, T

Purpose

Controls the position of print on the page. These settings link to the active document and save to disk.

Use this command before printing with the File Print command.

Procedures

1. Activate the document whose print settings you want to adjust.

2. Press Alt, F, T or click the File menu and select the Page SeTup command.

3. You can enter a Header or Footer to appear on every page. In addition to the actual text, you can enter the following codes in any combination:

Code	Effect
&&	Prints an ampersand.
&B	Prints boldface.
&C	Centers text.
&D	Prints the current date.
&F	Prints the document's name.

&I	Prints italic.
&L	Aligns text flush left.
&P	Prints the page number.
&P+*number*	Prints the page number added to a number.
&P-*number*	Prints the page number minus a number.
&R	Aligns text flush right.
&T	Prints the current time.

4. Change the Left, Right, Top and Bottom margins, which are in inches, if you want. You can use decimal fractions.

   Turn on Row & Column Headings to print the Row numbers and Column letters on each page.

   Turn on Gridlines to print horizontal and vertical lines along the rows and columns on each page.

5. Press Enter or click OK. Your settings link with the document and save.

File Print

Alt, F, P or Alt+Ctrl+Shift+F2 or Ctrl+Shift+F12

Purpose

Prints the active document.

Procedures

1. Activate the document you want to print.

2. Prepare worksheets for printing by using the Options Set Page Break and Options Set Print Area commands.

   Use the File PRinter Setup and File Page SeTup commands to adjust your printer options.

4. Press Alt, F, P, Alt+Ctrl+Shift+F2, or Ctrl+Shift+F12 or click the File menu and select the Print command.

The current printer setting appears in the dialog box. To use a different printer, press Esc to cancel, use the File PRinter Setup command to select a different printer option, then repeat this step.

5. Print by pressing Enter or clicking OK.

Notes

In the Print screen, you can specify the following print options:

- Enter the number of Copies you want to print (the default is 1).

- Choose between printing All page or selected pages. If the latter, enter From what starting page To what ending page.

- Turn on Draft Quality to print with lower resolution but greater speed.

- You can choose to print the Sheet values but not the cell notes, the Notes alone, or Both the values and the notes.

- Select Preview and press Enter or click OK to see what the document looks like, and where page breaks will occur. This feature saves you time and paper. You can see the Next page, Previous page, Zoom (which magnifies a portion of the document for closer inspection), and Print (which prints the document as shown).

File Printer Setup

Alt, F, R

Purpose

Enables you to specify the printer and certain basic printing options.

Procedures

1. Press Alt, F, R or click the File menu and select the PRinter Setup command.

2. Select the Printer you want to use.

3. Select Setup for more options. The options
   displayed depend on the printer you select.

4. Make appropriate changes and then press Enter or
   click OK. Your settings save to disk, and you return
   to the first dialog box.

4. Press Enter or click OK.

File Record Macro

Alt, F, C

Purpose

Duplicates the Macro ReCord command, recording your
Excel actions in a macro file. This command makes it
easy to create and name macros, but gives you less
control over where the macro stores on a macro sheet
than the Macro Start Recorder command.

Procedure

1. Plan the macro you want to record.

2. Press Alt, F, C or click the File menu and select the
   ReCord Macro command.

3. Accept the suggested macro name (Record
   followed by a number) or type a different name.

4. Accept the suggested letter to assign the macro, or
   type a different letter to run the macro when you
   press Ctrl.

5. When you are ready, press Enter or click OK.

6. Go through the actions you want to record. If a
   macro sheet was open before you started, the macro
   records on the sheet starting at the top of the next
   completely empty column. Otherwise, Excel opens
   a new sheet and starts recording in cell A1.

7. When you finish, press Alt, F, C or click the Macro
   menu and select Stop ReCorder.

8. You can run the macro by holding down **Ctrl** and pressing the letter you assigned it or by using the **Macro Run** command.

9. Save the macro sheet before you exit Excel.

File Save

Alt, F, S or Alt+Shift+F2 or Shift+F12

Purpose

Saves a file to disk as you continue to work. If the file exists, saves immediately. Otherwise, brings up a dialog box offering saving options.

Procedure

Press **Alt, F, S**; **Alt+Shift+F2**; **Shift+F12**, or click the File menu and select Save.

If the file exists on disk, the revised version replaces the disk version on-screen. If the file does not exist on disk, this command is identical to File Save As.

Note

Save about every 15 minutes so that you lose no more than 15 minutes worth of work if your power source fails.

File Save As

Alt, F, A or Alt+F2 or F12

Purpose

Saves a file to disk. Always brings up a dialog box offering saving options. .Enables you to duplicate an existing document by saving it to a different file name.

Procedures

1. Press **Alt, F, A, Alt+F2,** or **F12** or click the File menu and select the Save As command. A dialog box appears.

2. To save under the suggested directory and file name, press **Enter** or click OK.

To save under a different directory and file name, type the name you want and press **Enter** or click OK.

Notes

Select **O**ptions and choose to save your file in one the following file formats:

Normal	The standard Excel format.
Text	Also called ASCII, which is the generic format for PCs.
CSV	Comma Separated Values. Like Text except it separates fields with commas rather than tabs.
SYLK	Used by other Microsoft worksheets.
WKS,	Used by Lotus 1-2-3 Release 1A.
WK1	Used by Lotus 1-2-3 Release 2.
DIF	Data Interchange Format. Used by programs such as Visicalc.
DBF 2	Used by dBASE II; and DBF 3, used by dBASE III.

Protect the file by assigning a **P**assword of up to 16 letters, numbers, and symbols. You cannot access your file unless you have the word.

Create **B**ackup Files to save the preceding version of your file on disk by renaming it with a .BAK extension.

When you finish, press **Enter** or click OK. The file is saved in accordance with your settings.

For periodic saving of an existing document under the default options, **F**ile **S**ave is faster.

File Save Workspace

Purpose

Saves the entire workspace. All open documents are saved in individual files, and the names, sizes, and positions of all windows are saved in a workspace file. You can retrieve all documents as they appeared when you issued the command by opening the workspace file.

Procedures

1. Press **Alt, F, W** or click the **F**ile menu and select Save **W**orkspace.

   A dialog box appears asking you to supply a file name. If this is a new file, Excel suggests the default name RESUME.XLW. If this is an existing file, Excel suggests the current name.

2. To accept the suggested name, press **Enter** or click OK. To use a different file name, type the name and then press **Enter** or click OK.

All open documents are saved individually, and the workspace information is saved in the new file you select. You can exit Excel, later restart, and reestablish your documents and workspace by selecting **F**ile **O**pen and the name of your workspace file.

Notes

A workspace file contains a list of the documents that were open when the file was created, not the documents themselves.

If you do not specify an extension for the workspace file, Excel automatically appends an .XLW extension.

File Unhide Window

Alt, F, U

Purpose

Lists all hidden windows. Makes the window you select visible, and appears only when all windows are hidden.

Procedures

To unhide a window:

1. Press **Alt, F, U** or click the **F**ile menu and select **U**nhide Window. A list of hidden windows appears.

2. Select the window you want to see, and press **Enter** or click OK. The window reappears.

To suppress a window's display:

Select the **W**indow **H**ide command.

Note

If a window is protected with the **O**ptions **P**rotect Document command, Excel asks for a password before hiding the window and before unhiding the window.

Format Alignment

Alt, T, A

Purpose

Sets the alignment of selected cells.

Procedures

1. Select the cells you want aligned. (To select the entire worksheet, press **Ctrl+Shift+space bar**.)

2. Press **Alt, T, A** or click the Forma**T** menu and select the **A**lignment command.

3. Select one of the following options:

General	Aligns text left, numbers right, and logical values and errors centered.
Left, Center, or Right	Aligns all types of cell contents left, centered or right.
Fill	Repeats the contents of the cell until the display is full (for example, 123 in a cell width of 9 displays as 123123123, but the actual value of 123 remains unaffected).

4. Press **Enter** or click OK.

Notes

The default alignment is General.

Blank cells that are part of a Fill range take on the display of the cells to their left. You can create a border with a character or mix of characters.

Format Border

Alt, T, B

Purpose

Adds lines, boxes, and shading to selected cells.

Procedure

1. Select the cells you want to affect. (To select the entire worksheet, press **Ctrl+Shift+space bar**.)

2. Press **Alt**, **T**, **B** or click the FormaT menu and select the Border command.

3. Select one or more of the following options:

Outline	Draws a rectangular box around the range of cells.
Left	Draws a line to the left of each cell.
Right	Draws a line to the right of each cell.

Top	Draws a line above each cell.
Bottom	Draws a line below each cell.
Shade	Shades each cell.

4. Press **Enter** or click OK.

Notes

The default is no border or shading.

Create a double underline in a row by assigning **T**op and **B**ottom borders and then narrowing the distance between the borders with the Forma**T** **R**ow Height command.

Format Cell Protection

Alt, T, P (full menus)

Purpose

Safeguards selected cells and their formulas. **O**ptions **P**rotect Document **C**ontents must be on.

Procedures

1. Select the cells you want to protect. (To select the entire worksheet, press **Ctrl+Shift+space bar**.)

2. Press **Alt, T, P** or click the Forma**T** menu and select the Cell **P**rotection command.

3. Turn on the **L**ocked option to prevent editing in the cell contents.

4. Turn on the **H**idden option to prevent the cells' formulas appearing in the formula bar and Info window.

5. Press **Enter** or click OK.

6. If your settings do not take effect (that is, if you can alter a **L**ocked cell or see the formula in a **H**idden cell), select the **O**ptions **P**rotect Document command and turn on **C**ontents.

Note

The default is Locked cells.

Format Column Width

Alt, T, C

Purpose

Sets the display width of selected columns, and does not affect how much data the columns can hold.)

Procedures

1. Select at least one cell from each of the columns you want to change. (To change the width of all columns in the worksheet, select one entire row by pressing **Shift+space bar**.)

2. Press **Alt, T, C** or click the FormaT menu and select the Column Width command.

3. To specify a new column width, type the number of characters you want to appear in a cell, which can be 0 (which hides the columns from view) to 255.

   Your number can include decimal fractions, which represent fractions of a character. To reset the columns to the Standard Width (which is 8 characters), turn this option on instead.

5. Press **Enter** or click OK.

Notes

The default width is 8 characters.

If a column is too thin to display all data, you can view the data in the formula bar and the Info window.

If you are using a mouse, change a column's width dynamically by clicking the right border of the column's heading and dragging.

Format Font

Alt, T, F

Purpose

Changes the font for selected cells, chart text, or the entire document.

Procedures

To change the font:

1. Select the cells or chart text whose fonts you want to change.

2. Press **Alt, T, F** or click the Forma**T** menu and select the **F**ont command.

3. Select one of the four fonts.

4. Press **Enter** or click OK.

To change one of the four current fonts:

1. Press **Alt, T, F** or click the Forma**T** menu and select the **F**ont command.

2. Select the font number to change. (Changing font 1 changes the default font of the entire worksheet.)

3. Display extra font options by selecting F**O**nts.

4. Optionally select a different typeface from the list on your disk or display the typefaces offered by your printer by choosing **P**rinter Fonts.

5. Optionally select a different point size.

6. Optionally select a **B**old, **I**talic, **U**nderline, and/or Stri**K**eout style.

7. Press **Enter** or click OK.

Notes

The default font is font 1. For most systems, this font is initially Helvetica 10 point.

A document can use no more than four fonts.

Format Justify

Alt, T, J (full menus)

Purpose

Makes column text into a word-wrapped paragraph.

Procedures

1. Select a range with cells containing text as its leftmost column and blank cells in the rest of its columns.

2. Press Alt, T, J or click the FormaT menu and select Justify.

The text in the range's lower rows move to combine with the text in the upper rows to the extent permitted by the width of the range.

Note

Blank cells in the text column act as separators, creating multiple paragraphs instead of a single paragraph. The cells must be blank, not just cells containing spaces)

Format Legend

Alt, T, L (chart)

Purpose

Changes the position of the active chart's legend.

Procedures

1. Activate a chart with a legend.

2. Select the legend.

3. Press Alt, T, L or click the FormaT menu and select the Legend command.

4. Select to place the legend at the chart's Bottom, (top right) Corner, Top, or (right side, standing) Vertical.

5. To accept your settings and return to the chart, press **Enter** or click OK.

To accept your settings and move on to another chart Format command, select the **P**atterns or **F**ont option.

___
Note

The default is to position the legend vertically on the right side of the chart.

Format Main Chart

Alt, T, M (chart)

___
Purpose

Sets the active main chart's type and formatting.

___
Procedures

1. Press **Alt**, **T**, **M** or click the Forma**T** menu and select the **M**ain Chart command.

2. Select one of six chart types: **A**rea, **B**ar, **C**olumn, **L**ine, **P**ie, and **S**catter.

3. Depending on the chart type you select, you now have the following options:

Stacked	Creates a stacked chart.
Vary by Categories	Gives each data point in a single series a different color.
Drop Lines	Extends lines from the highest value in each category to the category axis.
100%	Shows the values in each category as percentages adding up to 100%.
Overlapped	Enables the % Ove**R**lap setting.
Hi-Lo Lines	Extends lines from the highest to lowest value in each category.

% OveRlap	If Overlapped is on, sets the extent to which markers within a cluster overlap. If it is off, sets the spacing between bars or columns within a cluster.
% Cluster SpacIng	Sets the spacing between clusters of bars or columns.
AnglE of First Pie	Slice (degrees) Sets the angle of the first edge of the first slice in a pie chart.

4. Press **Enter** or click OK.

___

Note

The default is a Column chart with all other options turned off and % Cluster SpacIng set at 50 percent.

Format Move

Alt, T, M (chart)

___

Purpose

Makes the active chart's objects moveable.

___

Procedures

1. Select the chart object you want to move.

2. Press **Alt, T, M** or click the FormaT menu and select Move.

3. Press the arrow keys to move the object in the direction you want. Press **Ctrl** plus the arrow keys to move in smaller increments.

4. When the object is where you want, press **Enter**.

If you are using a mouse, move a chart object by clicking and dragging it to where you want.

Format Number

Alt, T, N

Purpose

Sets the number, date, or time format of the values in selected cells.

Procedures

1. Select the cells whose numeric, date, or time values you want to set. (To select the entire worksheet, press **Ctrl+Shift+space bar**.)

2. Press **Alt**, **T**, **N** or click the Forma**T** menu and select the **N**umber command.

   The Format Number boxoffers you a list of 21 different formats, which include integers, scientific notation, currency, percentages, dates, and times.

3. Select one of these formats and press **Enter** or click OK.

Notes

The default number format is General.

You can create a custom format using the Format edit box. Excel adds your custom format to the Format Number list.

To remove a custom, select the format, and select **D**elete from the Format Number box. You cannot delete Excel formats.

Format Overlay

Alt, T, O (full menus) (chart)

Purpose

Sets an overlay chart's type and formatting.

Procedures

1. Activate a chart with an overlay.

2. Press **Alt**, **T**, **O** or click the Forma**T** menu and select the **O**verlay command.

The options appearing in the Forma**T** **M**ain Chart dialog box are offered here. Additionally, at the bottom of the dialog box are two new options:

First Series in Overlay Chart plots that series, and other series with higher plot order numbers, in the overlay after you enter a plot order number.

A**U**tomatic Series Distribution: If on, causes the data series to be divided evenly between the main chart and overlay. With an odd number of data series, the main chart incorporates the extra series.

3. Select the options you want.

4. Press **Enter** or click OK.

Note

The default for an overlay is a **L**ine chart with % Cluster Spac**I**ng set at 50%, **F**irst Series in Overlay Chart set to 2, A**U**tomatic Series Distribution turned on, and all other options turned off.

Format Patterns

Alt, T, P (chart)

Purpose

Sets the style, color, weight, and pattern of chart objects.

Procedures

1. Select the chart objects you want to affect. (To select all objects in the chart, use the **C**hart Select **C**hart command. To select the plot area, use the **C**hart Select Plot **A**rea command.)

2. Press **Alt**, **T**, **P** or click the Forma**T** menu and select the **P**atterns command.

The options vary depending on the selected objects.

3. Choose from the following options:

Style

Sets the line style of the axes, an object's border, or markers in a line chart.

Weight

Sets the weight of the axes, borders, lines, or arrow shafts.

Color Fore-
ground
Color/Back-
ground Color

Sets the color of the object, its border, its foreground, or its background.

Pattern

Sets the pattern of the axes, borders, areas, lines, or arrows.

Invisible

Suppresses the display of the selected object. (An object underneath becomes visible.)

Shadow

Creates a shadow at the bottom and right of text, legends, or the whole chart.

Automatic

For a data point or series, displays a color or pattern to differentiate each point or series. Otherwise sets the color or pattern to be the same as the window background.

INvert if Negative

Reverses the pattern for negative value markers.

Apply To All

Applies settings made for a selected data point to all data points in the chart.

Tick Mark Type,
Major/MinoR
Tick Labels

Sets the appearance of tickmarks on the axes and the position of the labels that appear next to the tickmarks.

ArrowHead

Sets the width, length and style of the selected arrowhead.

4. To accept your settings and return to the chart, press **Enter** or click OK. To accept your settings and move to another chart Forma**T** command, select the **P**atterns, **F**ont, **S**cale, or **T**ext option.

Format Row Height

Alt, T, R

Purpose

Sets the height of selected rows.

Procedures

1. Select at least one cell from each of the rows whose height you want to change. (To change the height of all rows in the worksheet, select one entire column by pressing Ctrl+space bar.)

2. Press **Alt**, **T**, **R** or click the Forma**T** menu and select the **R**ow Height command.

3. To specify a new row height, type the height's point size (72 points = 1 inch), which can range from 0 (which hides the rows from view) to 409.

   Your number can include decimal fractions, which represent fractions of a point.

   To reset the rows to the **S**tandard Height, (which varies depending on the largest font in the rows' cells), turn this option on.

5. Press **Enter** or click OK. The rows' heights reflect your settings.

Notes

The default row height for the default font (Helvetica 10 point) is 13 points.

If you are using a mouse, change a row's height dynamically by clicking the bottom border of the row's heading and dragging.

Format Scale

Purpose

Defines the active chart's axes settings.

Procedures

1. Select either the category axis or value axis.

2. Press **Alt, T, S** or click the Forma**T** menu and select the **S**cale command.

   If you select the category axis, six options appear. Value Axis **C**rosses at Category Number, which specifies the number of the category at which the Value axis crosses the Category axis (usually 1); Number of Categories Between Tick **L**abels; Number of Categories Between Tick Mar**K**s; Value Axis Crosses **B**etween Categories; Categories in **R**everse Order, which displays categories from right to left; and Value Axis **C**rosses at **M**aximum Category, which makes the Value axis cross the Category axis at the last category.

   If you select the Value axis, eight options appear. Set Mi**N**imum and Ma**X**imum values the chart will display; M**A**jor Unit and M**I**nor Unit for the distance between major and minor tickmarks; Category Axis **C**rosses At for the value at which the Category axis crosses the Value axis; whether **L**ogarithmic Scale should be used calculating the preceding settings; **R**everse Order, which displays values in ascending order; and Category Axis Crosses at **M**aximum Value, which makes the Value axis cross the Category axis at the last category.

3. To accept your settings and return to the chart, press **Enter** or click OK. To accept your settings and move to another chart Forma**T** command, select the **P**atterns or **F**ont option.

Format Size

Alt, T, Z (chart)

Purpose

Enables you to resize chart text objects.

Procedures

1. Select the chart object you want to resize.

2. Press **Alt**, **T**, **Z** or click the Forma**T** menu and select Si**Z**e.

3. Press the arrow keys to resize the object in the dimensions you want. Pressing **Ctrl** plus the arrow keys resizes in smaller increments.

4. When the object is the correct size, press **Enter**.

If you are using a mouse, resize a chart object by clicking and dragging its black selection squares.

Format Text

Alt, T, T (chart)

Purpose

Sets a chart's text's horizontal and vertical alignment, orientation, border size, and so on.

Procedures

1. Select the text you want to affect.

2. Press **Alt**, **T**, **T** or click the Forma**T** menu and select the **T**ext command.

3. Select a horizontal alignment and a vertical alignment.

4. To accept your settings and return to the chart, press **Enter** or click OK.

5. To accept the settings and use another chart Forma**T** command, select **P**atterns or **F**ont.

Notes

In the Format Text box, you can specify these options:

- Turn on **V**ertical Text to stack the text so it reads from top to bottom instead of left to right.

- Turn on **A**utomatic Text to restore text created with the **C**hart Attach **T**ext command and then revised to its original state.

- Turn on A**U**tomatic Size to resize the text border so that it always fits exactly around the text.

- If the text is attached to a data point, optionally turn on **S**how Value to replace the text with the data point's value.

- If the text is attached to a data point or series, optionally turn on S**H**ow Key to display the point or series' pattern next to the text.

Formula Apply Names

Alt, R, A

Purpose

Replaces references with designated names via the Fo**R**mula **C**reate Names and Fo**R**mula **D**efine Name commands.

Procedures

1. Select the range whose references you want to replace with names. If you do not select a range, references replace throughout the worksheet.

2. Press **Alt**, **R**, **A** or click the Fo**R**mula menu and select the **A**pply Names command.

   All existing names in the active worksheet appear in the Apply **N**ames box.

3. Highlight the names you want to apply by pressing **Ctrl** plus the up- and down-arrow keys, and then press the space bar or press **Shift** and click each name you want.

4. Press **Enter** or click OK.

Notes

In the Apply **N**ames box, you can change these options:

Ignore Relative/Absolute replaces references regardless of their respective types.

Use Row and Column Names applies names to references that are not exact matches. If you then select **O**ptions, you can set whether to Omit **C**olumn Name if Same Column, Omit **R**ow Name if Same Row, and display a cell reference replaced by both a row-oriented name and column-oriented name in Ro**W** Column or Column Row order.

Formula Create Names

Alt, R, C or Ctrl+Shift+F3 (full menus)

Purpose

Names areas of a worksheet with the text at the specified edges of the areas.

Procedures

1. Enter the names you want to assign to areas in the worksheet in the top row, left column, bottom row, and/or right column of the areas. (For example, to name all cells in a column, enter the name at the top or bottom of the area's column.) Names must begin with a letter, and can contain letters, digits, underlines (_), and periods (.), and can be up to 255 characters.

2. Select the areas.

3. Press **Alt**, **R**, **C** or **Ctrl+Shift+F3** or click the Fo**R**mula menu and select the **C**reate Names command.

4. Select **T**op Row, **L**eft Column, **B**ottom Row, and/or **R**ight Column to name each area with the text at its top, left, bottom, and/or right, respectively.

4. Press **Enter** or click OK.

Formula Define Name

Alt, R, D or Ctrl+F3

Purpose

Names ranges, a value, or formula. Enables you to edit and delete existing names.

Procedures

To name a range:

1. Select the range(s) you want to name.

2. Press **Alt, R, D** or **Ctrl+F3** or click the Fo**R**mula menu and select the **D**efine Name command.

   All existing names in the active worksheet appear in the Names in **S**heet box. The selected range's reference appears in **R**efers To box.

3. Name the selected range by typing a name in the **N**ame box. (Names must begin with a letter, can contain letters, digits, underlines (_), and periods (.), and can be up to 255 characters.)

   If you do not select a range, the text in the active cell appears in the **N**ame box. If the cell is blank, text in the cell to its left or top appears. Accept the name, or type a name for the cell.

   You can ignore what appears and type a new cell reference, or a value or formula, in the **R**efers To box. (Rather than use a static value such as 5 percent to represent an interest rate in the worksheet, type **5%** in the Refers To box and *Interest_Rate* in the Name box. Then use *Interest_Rate* in your formulas instead of 5 percent.)

4. When you finish, press Enter or click OK.

To revise an existing name or reference:

1. Select the range.

2. Press **Alt, R, D** or **Ctrl+F3** or click the Fo**R**mula menu and select the **D**efine Name command.

3. Make editing changes.

4. Press **Enter** or click OK.

To delete a name from the Names in Sheet list:

1. Select the name.

2. Press **Alt, R, D** or **Ctrl+F3** or click the FoRmula menu and select the Define Name command.

3. Select Delete.

4. Press **Enter** or click OK.

Formula Find

Alt, R, F or Shift+F5

Purpose

Finds the next occurrence of specified text or numbers.

Procedures

1. Optionally select the range whose contents you want to search. If you do not select a range, Excel searches the entire worksheet.

2. Press **Alt, R, F** or **Shift+F5** or click the FoRmula menu and select the Find command.

3. Type what you want to find in the Find What box. (You can use the DOS wildcards ? and *.)

4. Choose to search in Formulas (cell contents as they appear in the formula bar), Values (cell contents as they appear in the cell), or Notes.

5. Select WHole to require matches to consist of the entire cell, or Part to also find occurrences that are only part of longer text or number sequences.

6. Set the search to proceed by ROws or Columns.

7. Press **Enter** or click OK.

8. To find the next occurrence, press **F7**. To find the preceding occurrence, press **F8**.

9. Repeat Step 8 to find all occurrences. Excel advises you when no more messages are found.

Notes

> To find a question mark (?) or asterisk (*), precede the character with a tilde (~).
>
> See also the FoRmula REplace command.

Formula Goto

Alt, R, G or F5

Purpose

> Moves to the specified named area and selects it.

Procedures

> 1. Press Alt, R, G or click the Formula menu and select the Goto command.
>
> 2. All existing names in the active worksheet appear in the Goto box. Optionally select a name. It appears in the Reference box.
>
> 3. Optionally type a new reference in the Reference box. (If the area is in another worksheet, first type the name of the worksheet and an exclamation point, then the reference.)
>
> 4. When the area appears in the Reference box, press Enter or click OK. Excel jumps to the area and selects it. Also, your preceding area appears in the Reference box.
>
> 5. To return to the area you just left, repeat Step 1 and Step 4.

Formula Note

Alt, R, N or Shift+F2

Purpose

> Enables you to add, view, edit, and delete notes in a cell. The notes appear only in this command's dialog box, the Info window, and optionally in worksheet printouts.

Procedures

To add or edit a note:

1. Move to the cell you want to work with.

2. Press Alt, R, N or Shift+F2 or click the FoRmula menu and select the Note command.

   The reference of the active cell appears in the Cell box. Optionally enter a new reference to work with a different cell.

   The text of a note associated with the cell appears in the Note box.

3. Add text or edit the existing text in this box.

4. Apply your note additions or revisions by selecting Add. New notes appears with all other worksheet notes in the Notes in Sheet box.

5. Press Enter or click OK.

To delete a note:

1. Move to the cell you want to work with.

2. Press Alt, R, N or Shift+F2 or click the FoRmula menu and select the Note command.

3. Select the note from the Notes in Sheet box.

4. Select Delete.

5. Press Enter or click OK.

Note

Selecting Cancel closes the dialog box, but does not cancel changes you made while in the dialog box.

Formula Paste Function

Alt, R, T or Shift+F3

Purpose

Lists all worksheet formulas, and inserts the selected formula (and optionally its arguments) in the formula bar.

Procedures

1. Press **Alt**, **R**, **T** or **Shift+F3** or click the Fo**R**mula menu and select the Pas**T**e Function command.

2. All names in the active worksheet appear alphabetically. Select the name you want, or jump to a formula by pressing its beginning letter.

3. Press **Enter** or click OK to insert only the formula in the function bar. If you want both the formula and the names of its arguments inserted, select Paste **A**rguments and press **Enter** or click OK.

4. The formula appears in the function bar. If you chose to insert only the formula, insert the appropriate arguments. If you inserted both the formula and the argument names, replace the argument placeholders with the appropriate arguments.

Note

If a function has more than one form and Paste **A**rguments is on, a **S**elect Arguments box appears and prompts you to select arguments.

Formula Paste Name

Alt, R, P or F3

Purpose

Lists all worksheet names, and inserts the selected name in the formula bar. Can also insert the list of names and their references in the worksheet. Use this command only when the worksheet contains names.

Procedures

1. Press **Alt**, **R**, **P** or **F3** or click the Fo**R**mula menu and select the **P**aste Name command.

2. All names in the active worksheet appear alphabetically. Select the name you want, or jump to a formula by pressing its beginning letter.

3. To insert the selected name in the function bar, press **Enter** or click OK.

4. To insert a list of all the names and their references in the worksheet starting at the active cell, select Paste **L**ist.

Formula Reference

Alt, R, R or F4

Purpose

Switches selected references in the formula bar from relative to absolute, absolute to mixed, and mixed to relative.

Procedures

1. Move to the formula you want to change, press **F2**, and select the reference(s) you want to change.

2. Press **Alt**, **R**, **R** or **F4** or click the FoRmula menu and select **R**eference. The following results occur for the following reference types:

   A1 (relative) becomes A1 (absolute)
   A1 (absolute) becomes A$1 (mixed)
   A$1 (mixed) becomes $A1 (mixed)
   $A1 (mixed) becomes A1 (relative)

3. Repeat Step 2 until you get the results you want.

Formula Replace

Alt, R, E (full menus)

Purpose

Searches for specified text or numbers and replaces them with different text or numbers.

Procedures

1. Optionally use the File Save command to preserve the current version of the worksheet.

2. Optionally select the range whose contents you want to search and replace. If you do not select a range, Excel searches the entire worksheet.

3. Press Alt, R, E or click the FoRmula menu and select REplace.

4. Type what you want to replace in the Find What box. (Use the DOS wildcards ? and *.)

5. Type the replacement text in the With box.

6. Select WHole to require matches to consist of the entire cell, or Part to replace occurrences that are only part of longer text or number sequences.

7. Set the search to proceed by ROws or Columns.

8. To find the next occurrence, select Find Next. To find the previous occurrence, press and hold Shift and select Find Next.

9. To replace the current occurrence and then find the next occurrence, select Replace. Continue this procedure to replace all further occurrences. When all occurrences have been found, Excel displays the message No match.

10. Select Replace All to replace text automatically. (Check the worksheet immediately afterwards. If you do not like the results, select Edit Undo Replace.)

11. When you finish, press Enter or click OK.

Note

See also FoRmula Find.

Formula Select Special

Purpose

Selects all cells that fit a specified description.

Procedures

1. Select the range you want to match. If you do not select a range, Excel searches the entire worksheet.

2. Press **Alt**, **R**, **S** or click the Fo**R**mula menu and select the **S**elect Special command.

3. Choose to select cells containing **N**otes, **C**onstants, Fo**R**mulas (formula N**U**mbers, **T**ext, **L**ogicals and/or **E**rrors), or **B**lanks.

   or

   Select Current Regi**O**n (the cells forming a rectangular range around the active cell), Current **A**rray (an array containing the active cell), Ro**W** Differences (cells different from the cell intersecting their row and the active cell's column), Colu**M**n Differences (cells different from the cell intersecting their column and the active cell's row.

   or

   Select **P**recedents or **D**ependents (cells that support or depend on the selected cells) at the D**I**rect Only level or at All Le**V**els.

4. Press **Enter** or click OK.

Notes

Use the following keyboard shortcuts to bypass the dialog box:

Ctrl+?	Notes
Ctrl+/	Current Array
Ctrl+	Ro**W** Differences
Ctrl+|	Colu**M**n Differences

Ctrl+[	Precedents Direct Only
Ctrl+{	Precedents All LeVels
Ctrl+]	Dependents DIrect Only
Ctrl+}	Dependents All LeVels

Gallery Area

Alt, G, A (chart)

Purpose

Shows the area formats available and enables you to select a format to apply to the active chart.

Procedures

1. Press **Alt, G, A** or click the **G**allery menu and select the **A**rea command.

2. Five area formats are displayed: a basic area chart, a 100% area chart, a chart with drop lines, a chart with gridlines, and a chart with areas labeled.

3. To see the formats for the other chart types on the **G**allery menu, select **N**ext or **P**revious.

4. Select the format you want; then press **Enter** or click OK. The format applies to the active chart.

Gallery Bar

Alt, G, B (chart)

Purpose

Shows the bar formats available and enables you to select a format to apply to the active chart.

Procedures

1. Press **Alt, G, B** or click the **G**allery menu and select the **B**ar command.

2. Seven bar formats are displayed: a basic area chart, a chart for one series with varied patterns, a stacked

chart, an overlapped chart, a 100% stacked chart, a chart with vertical gridlines, and a chart with value labels.

3. To see the formats for other chart types on the Gallery menu, select Next or Previous.

4. Select the format you want, select it; then press Enter or click OK.

Gallery Column

Alt, G, C (chart)

Purpose

Shows the column formats available and enables you to select a format to apply to the active chart.

Procedures

1. Press Alt, G, C or click the Gallery menu and select the Column command.

2. Eight column formats are displayed: a basic column chart, a chart for one series with varied patterns, a stacked chart, an overlapped chart, a 100% stacked chart, a chart with horizontal gridlines, a chart with value labels, and a step chart.

3. To see the formats for the other chart types on the Gallery menu, select Next or Previous.

4. Select the format you want; then press Enter or click OK. The format applies to the active chart.

Gallery Combination

Alt, G, M (full menus) (chart)

Purpose

Shows the combination formats available and enables you to select a format to apply to the active chart.

Procedures

1. Press **Alt**, **G**, **M** or click the **G**allery menu and select the Co**M**bination command.

2. Five combination formats are displayed: a column chart overlaid by a line chart, a column chart overlaid by a line chart with independent scale, a line chart overlaid by a line chart with independent scale, an area chart overlaid by a column chart, and a bar chart overlaid by a line chart containing three data series.

3. To see the other formats on the **G**allery menu, select **N**ext or **P**revious.

4. Select the format you want; then press **Enter** or click OK. The format applies to the active chart.

Gallery Line

Alt, G, L (chart)

Purpose

Shows the line formats available and enables you to select a format to apply to the active chart.

Procedures

1. Press **Alt**, **G**, **L** or click the **G**allery menu and select the **L**ine command.

2. Eight line formats are displayed: a lines and markers chart, a lines chart, a markers chart, a lines and markers with horizontal gridlines chart, a lines and markers with horizontal and vertical gridlines chart, a lines and markers with logarithmic scale and gridlines chart, a hi-lo chart with markers and hi-lo lines, and a high-low-close chart.

3. To see the other formats on the **G**allery menu, select **N**ext or **P**revious.

4. Select the format you want; then press **Enter** or click OK. The format applies to the active chart.

Gallery Pie

Alt, G, P (chart)

Purpose

Shows the pie formats available and enables you to select a format to apply to the active chart.

Procedures

1. Press **Alt**, **G**, **P** or click the **G**allery menu and select the **P**ie command.

2. Six pie formats are displayed: a basic pie chart, a chart that uses the same pattern on all wedges and labels the categories, an exploded pie chart with the first wedge exploded, an exploded pie chart with all wedges exploded, a chart with category labels, and a chart with values labels expressed as percentages.

3. To see the other formats on the **G**allery menu, select **N**ext or **P**revious.

4. Select the format you want; then press **Enter** or click OK. The format applies to the active chart.

Gallery Preferred

Alt, G, R (full menus) (chart)

Purpose

Applies the format you select with the **G**allery Se**T** Preferred command to the active chart.

Procedures

Press **Alt**, **G**, **R** or click the **G**allery menu and select **P**referred. The default format applies to the active chart.

Gallery Scatter

Alt, G, S (chart)

Purpose

Shows the scatter formats available and enables you to select a format to apply to the active chart.

Procedures

1. Press **Alt, G, S** or click the **G**allery menu and select the **S**catter command.

2. Five scatter formats are displayed: a chart with markers only, a chart with markers from the same series connected by lines, a chart with markers and horizontal and vertical gridlines, a chart with semi-logarithmic gridlines, and a chart with log-log gridlines.

3. To see the other formats on the **G**allery menu, select **N**ext or **P**revious.

4. Select the format you want; then press **Enter** or click OK. The format applies to the active chart.

Gallery Set Preferred

Alt, G, T (full menus) (chart)

Purpose

Changes the default chart format to one you specify.

Procedures

1. Select a chart format you want to make the default.

2. Press **Alt**, **G**, **T** or click the **G**allery menu and select the Se**T** Preferred command. Select the **G**allery P**R**eferred command to apply your selected format to the active chart.

Note

The format is lost when you exit Excel, unless you use the File Save Workspace command to save the workspace.

Help About

Alt, H, A

Purpose

Shows Excel's version number and copyright date, the amount of conventional and expanded memory currently available, and whether a math co-processor chip is installed.

Procedures

1. Press Alt, H, A or click the Help menu and select About.

2. Read the information. Press Enter or click OK.

Help Feature Guide

Alt, H, F

Purpose

Provides a guided tour of Excel's advanced features for those who are familiar with electronic spreadsheets and basic Excel commands.

Procedures

1. Press Alt, H, F or click the Help menu and select Feature Guide.

2. Excel prompts you to save open documents. Press Enter or click OK to save each document.

3. Seven pictorial options appear:

What's in the Feature Guide	Provides an overview of the Guide.
Basic Mechanics	Teaches how to navigate, select data, use menus and dialog boxes, copy data, save documents, and print documents.
Multiple Windows	Covers using and linking multiple windows, and managing the workspace.
Charts	Shows how to customize charts, and create special effects such as combination charts.
Worksheet Formatting	Explores how to create professional-looking reports.
Macros	Explains how to automate your work.
Auditing and Documenting	Details how to use cell notes, range names, and other features to aid checking the integrity of your data and formulas.

Press the number of the topic you want.

4. Quit by pressing **Q** if you are at the Main Menu, or **F1, Q** if you are in a lesson.

5. When you exit the Guide, Excel reopens your documents and restores your workspace.

Note

See also **H**elp **T**utorial.

Help Index

Alt, H, I

Purpose

Offers an alphabetical list of on-line documentation.

Procedures

1. Press **Alt, H, I** or click the **H**elp menu and select **I**ndex.

2. Scroll the list by pressing **PgUp** and **PgDn**, or by clicking the scroll bars. Print the list by pressing **Alt, P** or by clicking the **P**rint command.

3. Use the up- and down-arrow keys to highlight a topic and press **Enter**, or click the topic.

4. Press **Alt, N** or click the **N**ext command to cycle through topics. Press **Alt, B** or click the **B**ack command to cycle back. Press **Alt, I** or click the **I**ndex command to return to the Help Index at any time.

5. When you finish, press **Esc** to exit **H**elp.

Help Keyboard

Alt, H, K

Purpose

Offers an on-line keyboard documentation.

Procedures

1. Press **Alt, H, K** or click the **H**elp menu and select **K**eyboard.

2. The following topics appear: Function Keys, Control Key Shortcuts, Worksheet Keys, Chart Keys, Formula Bar Keys, and Menu, Command, Dialog Box Keys. Print the list by pressing **Alt, P** or by clicking the **P**rint command.

3. Use the up- and down-arrow keys to highlight a topic and press **Enter**, or click the topic. Press **PgUp** and **PgDn**, or click the scroll bars to scroll the explanatory text.

4. Press **Alt**, **N** or click the **N**ext command to cycle through the topics. Press **Alt**, **B** or click the **B**ack command to cycle back. Press **Alt**, **I** or click the **I**ndex command to jump to the Help Index.

5. When you finish, press **Esc** to exit **H**elp.

Help Lotus 123

Alt, H, L

Purpose

Provides the Excel equivalent of 1-2-3 commands.

Procedures

1. Press **Alt**, **H**, **L** or click the **H**elp menu and select **L**otus 123.

2. Type a 1-2-3 key sequence in the dialog box (**/FSR** to save a file) and press **Enter**.

3. Excel moves you to on-line **H**elp that discusses the equivalent Excel command (**F**ile **S**ave **A**s). Scroll the text by pressing **PgUp** and **PgDn**, or by clicking the scroll bars.

4. Cycle to the next topic by pressing **Alt**, **N** or clicking the **N**ext command. Cycle back by pressing **Alt**, **B** or clicking the **B**ack command. Jump to the Help Index by pressing **Alt**, **I** or clicking the **I**ndex command. Print the text by pressing **Alt**, **P** or by clicking the **P**rint command.

5. When you finish, press **Esc** to exit **H**elp.

Help Multiplan

Alt, H, M

Purpose

Provides the Excel equivalent of Multiplan commands.

Procedures

1. Press **Alt**, **H**, **M** or click the **Help** menu and select **M**ultiplan.

2. Type a Multiplan key sequence in the dialog box (**TS** to save a file) and press **Enter**.

3. Excel moves you to the on-line **Help** that discusses the equivalent Excel command (**F**ile **S**ave **A**s). Scroll the text by pressing **PgUp** and **PgDn**, or by clicking the scroll bars.

4. Cycle to the next topic by pressing **Alt**, **N** or clicking the **N**ext command. Cycle back by pressing **Alt**, **B** or clicking the **B**ack command. Jump to the Help Index by pressing **Alt**, **I** or clicking the **I**ndex command. Print the text by pressing **Alt**, **P** or by clicking the **P**rint command.

5. When you finish, press **Esc** to exit **Help**.

Help Tutorial

Alt, H, T

Purpose

Runs an on-line step-by-step tutorial that goes through Excel's basic features.

Procedures

1. Press **Alt**, **H**, **T** or click the **Help** menu and select **T**utorial.

2. Excel prompts you to press **Enter** or click OK to save each document.

3. Six pictorial options appear: How to Use This Tutorial, Microsoft Excel Introduction, MDNM/. Worksheets, Charts, Databases, and Macros.

   Press the number of the topic you want.

4. Press Q to quit if you are at the Main Menu, or F1, Q if you are in a lesson.

5. When you exit the Tutorial, Excel reopens your documents and restores your workspace.

Note

See also the Help Feature Guide command.

Info Cell

Alt, I, C (full menus)

Purpose

Toggles the display of the active cell's reference in the Info window.

Procedure

Press Alt, I, C or click the Info menu and select Cell.

Notes

The Info window default is to turn on the cell reference.

To bring up the Info window, select the Window Show Info command.

Info Dependents

Alt, I, D (full menus)

Purpose

Toggles the display of the active cell's dependents in the Info window.

Procedure

1. Press **Alt**, **I**, **D** or click the Info menu and select Dependents.

   Excel prompts you to choose between two display options. Direct Only lists cells containing formulas that refer directly to the active cell. All Levels lists cells that indirectly refer to the active cell (refer to the cell's dependents, and refer to the dependent cells' dependents, and so on).

2. Select one of the preceding options, and press **Enter** or click OK.

Notes

The Info window default is dependents information off.

To bring up the Info window, select the **W**indow **S**how Info command.

Info Format

Alt, I, T (full menus)

Purpose

Toggles the display of the active cell's formatting information in the Info window.

Procedure

Press **Alt**, **I**, **T** or click the Info menu and select Forma**T**.

If Forma**T** was turned on, the formatting disappears from the Info window.

If Forma**T** was turned off, the active cell's number, alignment, font, border, and shading formats now appear in the Info window.

Notes

The Info window default is to turn formatting information off.

To bring up the Info window, select the **W**indow **S**how Info command.

See also the Forma**T** menu commands.

Info Formula

Alt, I, R (full menus)

Purpose

Toggles the display of the active cell's formula in the Info window.

Procedure

Press **Alt**, **I**, **R** or click the **I**nfo menu and select Fo**R**mula.

Notes

The Info window default is to turn formula information on.

To bring up the Info window, select the **W**indow **S**how Info command.

Info Names

Alt, I, M (full menus)

Purpose

Toggles the display of names associated with the active cell or with ranges that the active cell is part of in the Info window.

Reminders

This command appears in the Info window only when operating in Full **M**enus.

To bring up the Info window, select the **W**indow **S**how Info command.

Procedure

Press Alt, I, M or click the Info menu and select NaMes.

Notes

The Info window default is to turn off name information.

For information on creating names, see also the FoRmula Define Name and FoRmula Create Names commands.

Info Note

Alt, I, N (full menus)

Purpose

Toggles the display of a note associated with the active cell in the Info window.

Procedure

Press Alt, I, N or click the Info menu and select Note.

Notes

The Info window default is to turn on note information.

To bring up the Info window, select the Window Show Info command.

See also FoRmula Note.

Info Precedents

Alt, I, P (full menus)

Purpose

Toggles the display of the active cell's precedents in the Info window.

Procedure

Press **Alt, I, P** or click the Info menu and select Precedents.

If Precedents was turned off, Excel prompts you to choose Direct Only, which lists the cells the formula in the active cell refers to directly, or All Levels, which lists the cells the active cell refers to indirectly. Select one of the options, and press **Enter** or click OK.

Notes

The Info window default is precedents information off.

To bring up the Info window, select the Window Show Info command.

Info Protection

Alt, I, O (full menus)

Purpose

Toggles the display of the active cell's protection status in the Info window

Procedure

Press **Alt, I, O** or click the Info menu and select PrOtection.

Notes

The Info window default is protection information off.

To activate the Info window, select the Window Show Info command.

See also FormaT Cell Protection and Options Protect Document commands.

Info Value

Alt, I, V (full menus)

Purpose

Toggles the display of the active cell's value in the Info window.

Procedure

Press **Alt**, **I**, **V** or click the **I**nfo menu and select **V**alues.

Notes

The Info window default is value information off.

To activate the Info window, select the **W**indow **S**how Info command.

Macro Absolute Record

Alt, M, A (full menus)

Purpose

Records macro cell references as absolute references.

Procedure

Press **Alt**, **M**, **A** or click the **M**acro menu and select **A**bsolute Record.

Notes

This option is the default.

This command appears only when you select **M**acro Rel**A**tive Record when operating in Full **M**enus. You can select this command before and during macro recording.

Macro Record

Purpose

Records your Excel actions in a macro file. Although this command makes it easy to create and name macros, you have less control over the placement of the macro on a macro sheet than when you use the Macro Start Recorder command.

Procedures

1. Plan the macro you want to record.

2. Press **Alt**, **M**, **C** or click the **M**acro menu and select the Re**C**ord command.

3. Accept the suggested macro name (`Record` followed by a number) or type a different name.

4. Accept the suggested letter to assign the macro, or type a different letter.

5. When you are ready, press **Enter** or click OK. `Recording` appears in the status bar.

6. Go through the actions you want to record. If a macro sheet was open before you started, the macro records on the sheet starting at the top of the next completely empty column. Otherwise, Excel opens a new sheet and records starting in cell A1.

7. When you finish, press **Alt**, **M**, **C** again or click the **M**acro menu and select Stop Re**C**order.

8. You now can run the macro by pressing **Ctrl** plus the letter you assigned the macro, or by using the **M**acro **R**un command.

9. To permanently store the macro, save the macro sheet containing the macro before you exit Excel.

Notes

This command appears only when you are not recording a macro.

See also the Macro Functions section of this book.

Macro Relative Record

Alt, M, A (full menus)

Purpose

Records macro cell references as relative references.

Procedure

Press **Alt, M, A** or click the **M**acro menu and select Rel**A**tive Record.

Notes

The default is **A**bsolute Record.

This command appears only when you select **M**acro **A**bsolute Record when operating in Full **M**enus. You can select this command before and during macro recording.

Macro Run

Alt, M, R

Purpose

Lists all named macros on open macro sheets and runs the macro you select.

Procedures

1. Press **Alt, M, R** or click the **M**acro menu and select the Macro **R**un command.

2. Select the macro you want from the list, or type its name or the reference of its first cell in the Re**F**erence box.

3. Press **Enter** or click OK. The macro runs.

Note

A macro name consists of the macro sheet name, followed by an explanation point, and then the actual name.

Macro Set Recorder

Alt, M, T (full menus)

Purpose

Defines a range in a macro sheet for storing macros recorded with the Macro Start Recorder command.

Procedures

1. Activate a new or existing macro sheet.

2. Select the range in which to store the macro.

3. Press Alt, M, T or click the Macro menu and select SeT Recorder. The range is defined for macro storage. You now can use the Macro Start Recorder command to create a macro.

Macro Start Recorder

Alt, M, S (full menus)

Purpose

Records your Excel actions in a macro file. Although this command gives you more control over macro placement on a macro sheet, creating and naming the macro is more burdensome than when you use the Macro ReCord command.

Procedures

1. Plan the macro you want to record.

2. Activate a new or existing macro sheet.

3. Select the range in which to store the macro and select the Macro SeT Recorder command.

4. Activate the document in which you want to perform your actions.

5. Press Alt, M, S or click the Macro menu and select Start Recorder.

6. Go through the actions you want to record. The actions record in the range you define.

7. When you finish, press **Alt, M, C** again or click the **M**acro menu and select Stop Re**C**order.

8. You now can run the macro by using the **M**acro **R**un command.

9. To change the default macro name and its default **Ctrl** letter, use the Fo**R**mula **D**efine Name command.

10. To permanently store the macro, save the macro sheet containing the macro before you exit Excel.

Note

You also can write macros using the Macro Functions listed in the back portion of this book.

Macro Stop Recorder

Alt, M, C

Purpose

Ends a macro recording session.

Procedures

1. Press **Alt, M, C** or click the **M**acro menu and select Stop Re**C**order. The macro recording ends.

2. Select **M**acro **S**tart Recorder to resume recording. The macro recording continues from Step 1.

When you finish, repeat Step 1 again.

Options Calculate Document

Alt, Shift+O, N or Shift+F9 (shifted command)

Purpose

Forces calculation in the active document only.

Procedure

Press **Alt**, **O**, **N** or **Shift+F9** or press **Shift**, click the **O**ptions menu, and select Calculate Docume**N**t.

Options Calculate Now

Alt, O, N or F9

Purpose

Forces calculation in all open worksheets and charts.

Procedure

Press **Alt**, **O**, **N** or **F9** or click the **O**ptions menu and select Calculate **N**ow.

Note

This command is only necessary when you select the **M**anual option in the **O**ptions **C**alculation dialog box.

Options Calculation

Alt, O, C

Purpose

Controls how formulas calculate.

Procedures

1. Press **Alt**, **O**, **C** or click the **O**ptions menu and select **C**alculation.

2. Select one of three calculation options:

Automatic	Calculates all formulas that refer to a changed cell (the default).
Automatic except **T**ables	Makes tables the one exception because they tend to be especially slow in calculating.

Manual   Shuts automatic calculation off
                      entirely.

3. Optionally select iteration limits. Excel's defaults
   are 100 for Maximum Iterations and 0.001 for
   Maximum Charge.

4. Optionally turn on or off the following features:

   Update Remote   Controls the calculation of
   References   formulas referring to other
                        applications.

   Precision   Speeds calculations but limits
   as Displayed   their accuracy.

   1904 Date System   Sets how dates calculate.

5. When you finish, press Enter or click OK.

Options Display

Alt, O, D

Purpose

Sets whether the active worksheet displays formulas (as
opposed to values), gridlines, row and column headings,
and zero values. Excel's default is formula display off.

Procedures

1. Press Alt, O, D or click the Options menu and
   select Display.

2. Optionally select FoRmulas, which sets cells to
   display formulas if on, or the formulas resulting
   values if off.

3. Optionally select Gridlines, which displays lines
   along row and column boundaries if on, or no lines
   if off.

4. Optionally select Row & Column Headings, which
   displays letters across the top of the columns and
   numbers down the left side of the rows if on, no
   headings if off.

5. Optionally select Zero Values, which displays a 0 in cells with zero values if on, a blank cell if off.

6. You can select a color if Gridlines and Row & Column Headings is on and your system supports color.

7. When you finish, press Enter or click OK.

Options Freeze Panes

Alt, O, F (full menus)

Purpose

Stops the scrolling of the top and left panes of a divided worksheet with the Control Split command. This command keeps row or column titles stationary.

Procedure

Press Alt, O, F or click the Options menu and select Freeze Panes.

Options Full Menus

Alt, O, M (short menus)

Purpose

Sets menus to display all options.

Procedure

Press Alt, O, M or click the Options menu and select Full Menus.

Note

This command affects all menus.

Options Protect Document

Alt, O, P (full menus)

Purpose

Safeguards a document's cells. Optionally provides password protection.

Procedures

1. Press **Alt, O, P** or click the Options menu and select the Protect Document command.

2. Select Contents to enforce or rescind the cell locking or cell hiding settings in the FormaT Cell Protection dialog box.

3. Select Windows to protect or unprotect the document window screen position, size, and other characteristics.

4. To protect your settings, select Password and enter a word consisting of up to 16 letters, numbers, and symbols.

5. Press **Enter** or click OK.

Note

Make sure that you remember or store the password in a safe place. You cannot make further changes to a document unless you know the password.

Options Remove Page Break

Alt, O, B (full menus)

Purpose

Deletes manual page breaks.

Procedures

1. Position the cell pointer directly below or to the right of the page break you want to remove.

2. Press **Alt**, **O**, **B** or click the **O**ptions menu and select Remove Page **B**reak. The page break disappears.

Notes

This command appears only when the cell pointer is directly below or to the right of a manual page break.

This command works on manual page breaks only. You cannot remove automatic page breaks because locations shift in conjunction with printing settings and manual page breaks.

Options Set Page Break

Alt, O, B (full menus)

Purpose

Forces the printer to start a new page by inserting a code above and to the left of the worksheet's cell pointer. Excel does not limit the number of manual page breaks you can insert.

Procedures

1. Move to where you want to insert a page break.

2. Press **Alt**, **O**, **B** or click the **O**ptions menu and select Set Page **B**reak. Dashed lines appear above and to the left of the cell pointer.

Note

Use the **O**ptions Remove Page **B**reak command to remove manual page breaks.

Options Set Print Area

Alt, O, A

Purpose

Specifies the area of the worksheet you want printed.

Procedures

1. Select the worksheet area you want to print.

2. Press **Alt**, **O**, **A** or click the **O**ptions menu and select Set Print **A**rea. Dashed lines outline the print area, and Excel internally names the section Print_Area. Only this section of the worksheet prints when you select the **F**ile **P**rint command.

3. Repeat Steps 1 and 2 to define a new print area.

Note

Use the Fo**R**mula **D**efine Name command to remove (as opposed to redefine) a print area. This command deletes the name Print_Area.

Options Set Print Titles

Alt, O, T (full menus)

Purpose

Specifies title text for worksheet printing. As long as the columns or rows are adjacent, you can include text from anywhere in the worksheet. Text in a title cell prints near the top or to the left of every page that contains a worksheet cell in the same column or row.

Procedures

1. Enter the title text in the worksheet you want printed. Make sure that the text is in adjoining rows and columns.

2. Specify the print title. Using the keyboard, select entire rows by pressing **Shift+space bar** and then **Shift+up-** or **down-arrow**. Select entire columns by pressing **Ctrl+space bar** and then **Shift+left-** or **right-arrow**. Using the mouse, select entire rows and/or columns by clicking their headings, pressing **Shift**, and dragging.

3. Press **Alt**, **O**, **T** or click the **O**ptions menu and select Set Print **T**itles. Excel internally names the section Print_Titles.

Repeat Steps 1-3 to define new print titles.

Note

To remove (as opposed to redefine) the print specification, use the FoRmula Define Name command which deletes the name Print_Titles.

Options Short Menus

Alt, O, M (full menus)

Purpose

Sets menus to display only the most-used options, thus simplifying Excel for beginners.

Procedure

Press Alt, O, M or click the Options menu and select Short Menus.

Note

This command affects all menus.

Options Unfreeze Panes

Alt, O, F (full menus)

Purpose

Reverses the action of the Options Freeze Panes command, once again enabling scrolling.

Procedure

Press Alt, O, F or click the Options menu and select UnFreeze Panes.

Options Unprotect Document

Alt, O, P (full menus)

Purpose

Removes safeguards you created with the Options
Protect Document command. If the document is
password-protected, you must supply that password.

Procedures

1. Press Alt, O, P or click the Options menu and
   select UnProtect Document.

2. If the document is not password protected, you can
   alter the document.

   If the chart is password protected, Excel requests a
   password. Type the appropriate password, and press
   Enter or click OK. If your password is correct, you
   can alter the document.

   If your password is incorrect, Excel beeps and
   displays an error message. The document stays
   locked unless you supply the correct password.

Options Workspace

Alt, O, W (full menus)

Purpose

Determines decimal settings that apply to all documents
and the surrounding workspace.

Procedures

1. Press Alt, O, W or click the Options menu and
   select Workspace.

2. Select Fixed Decimal and enter the number of
   decimal places you want in the Places text box.
   (For example, if you select 2 decimal places, and
   then enter a cell value of 1111, Excel changes the
   number to 11.11. If you select -2 decimal-places,

Excel changes 1111 to 111100. This command does not affect numbers in which you manually insert a decimal point.

The default for this option is off, with Places set to 2 if on.

3. Turn on R1C1 to display headings and cell references in Row-Column format instead of Excel's default A1 format. (For example, the reference A1 becomes R1C1, B3 becomes R3C2, and so on.)

4. Select SCroll Bars to turn their display on or off. The default is on.

5. Select Status Bar to turn the status display at the bottom of the screen on and off. The default is on.

6. Select FoRmula Bar to turn the display/editing area at the top of documents on and off. The default is on.

7. Change the Alternate Menu key, which duplicates the Alt key's action of selecting the menu bar. The default is the slash (/) key.

8. Select Ignore Remote Requests to ignore or not ignore other Windows applications that make remote (DDE) requests to Excel. The default is off.

Window Activate Window

Alt, W, window#

Purpose

Lists open windows and enables you to select the active window.

Procedures

1. Press Alt, W or click the Window menu to display up to nine open windows.

2. Activate a particular window by typing the number to its left in the menu or by clicking the window.

Note

> If more than nine windows are open, use the **W**indow **M**ore Windows command.

Window Arrange All

Alt, W, A

Purpose

> Rearranges all on-screen windows to take maximum advantage of available space.

Procedure

> Press **Alt**, **W**, **A** or click the **W**indow menu and select **A**rrange All.

Note

> This command is most effective when used in combination with the Control **M**ove and Control **S**ize commands.

Window Hide

Alt, W, H (full menus)

Purpose

> Makes the active window invisible to free screen space. The window remains open, available to other documents with which it is linked.

Procedure

> Press **Alt**, **W**, **H** or click the **W**indow menu and select **H**ide. The window is hidden.

Notes

> The Info window does not display information about hidden windows.

Excel asks for a password before hiding or unhiding a window with the Options Protect Document command.

Window More Windows

Alt, W, M

Purpose

Lists the names of all windows, including those that scroll off the Window menu, and activates the window you select.

Procedures

1. Press Alt, W, M or click the Window menu and select the More Windows command.

2. Scroll through the list of open windows and select the one you want to make active.

3. Press Enter or click OK.

Note

This command appears only when you have more than nine windows open.

Window New Window

Alt, W, N

Purpose

Creates one or more additional windows for the active document. Enables you to work in one window while displaying other sections of the document in other windows.

Procedure

Press Alt, W, N or click the Window menu and select New Window. The additional window appears.

To create additional windows, repeat this procedure. The number of additional windows is limited only by your system's memory.

To move among windows, select the one you want from the Window menu or click the window.

Notes

To get synchronized scrolling, select the Control SpliT command.

Windows of the same document are numbered so that you can distinguish each window. Suppose that a document is named Report. When Window New Window is used for the first time, the document's original window is renamed Report:1 and its new window is named Report:2. The document name remains intact.

To create a new window for a new document, select the File New command.

Window Show Document

Alt, W, S (full menus)

Purpose

Makes the worksheet referred to by the Info window the active window.

Procedure

Press Alt, W, S or click the Window menu and select Show Document.

Notes

This command appears only when the Info window is the active window.

You can view simultaneously the Info window and the worksheet to which it refers by sizing them to fit together on-screen. This arrangement enables you to display information about a cell instantly by selecting the cell. Under these circumstances, Window Show Document does not "show" the document, but moves you to the visible worksheet.

Window Show Info

Alt, W, S or Ctrl+F2 (full menus)

Purpose

Displays the Info window, which displays information about the active worksheet or macro sheet.

Procedures

1. Press **Alt**, **W**, **S** or **Ctrl+F2** or click the **W**indow menu and select **S**how Info.

2. Read the information about the active cell's reference, formula, and notes.

3. Select the **I**nfo menu by pressing **Alt**, **I** or click on **I**nfo and select the appropriate commands to see more information.

4. Return to the active worksheet or macro sheet by selecting the **W**indow **S**how Document command.

Note

For more information on the Info window, see the **I**nfo menu commands.

Window Unhide

Alt, W, U (full menus)

Purpose

Lists all hidden windows and makes the window you select visible.

Procedures

1. Press **Alt**, **W**, **U** or click the **W**indow menu and select **U**nhide. A dialog box lists hidden windows.

2. Select the window you want to see, and press Enter or click OK. The window reappears on screen.

Note

For windows protected with the Options Protect Document command, Excel asks for a password before hiding and unhiding the window.

WORKSHEET FUNCTIONS

This section lists alphabetically and briefly describes all Excel worksheet functions. These functions are miniprograms that you can include in your worksheet formulas.

Functions take and pass back data through variables called *arguments*. Each function has its own list of arguments, which are enclosed in parentheses and directly follow the function name. In this book, if an argument appears in normal print, it is mandatory. If the argument is italicized, it is optional. If the argument is followed by an ellipsis (...), it is part of a repeatable series (functions can have up to 13 arguments).

ABS(*number*)

Returns the absolute value of a number.

ACOS(*number*)

Returns the arccosine of a number, in radians.

AND(*logical1*,*logical2*,...)

Returns TRUE if arguments are TRUE; otherwise FALSE.

AREAS(*reference*)

Produces the number of areas (ranges of cells or single cells) in a specified reference.

ASIN(*number*)

Returns the arcsine of a number, in radians.

ATAN(*number*)

Returns the arctangent of a number, in radians.

ATAN2(*x_number,y_number*)

Returns the arctangent of x and y coordinates, in radians.

AVERAGE(*number1,number2,...*)

Averages a group of numbers.

CELL(*type_of_info,reference*)

Depending on the *type_of_info* argument, returns a cell's column width. The row or column number in a specified *reference*; a 1 if a cell is locked, 0 if it is not locked; reference of the first cell in *reference* formatted as text; value of the first cell in *reference* or text value corresponding to a cell's format, label prefix, or type of contents.

Text values for formats include "G" for general, "F0" and "F2" for plain numbers, "CO" and "C2" for currency, "P0" and "P2" for percentages, "S2" for scientific notation, and "D1"-"D9" for date and time.

CHAR(*number*)

Produces an ASCII character corresponding to a number between 1 and 255.

CHOOSE(*index_number,value1,value2,...*)

Returns the value in a list corresponding to the number position specified by *index_number*.

CLEAN(*text*)

Returns the text resulting from removing all non-printable characters from a *text* string.

CODE(*text*)

Returns the ASCII code of the first character in a *text* string.

COLUMN(*reference*)

Produces the column number(s) of one or more columns you specify. If no column is specified, the column in which the function appears returns.

COLUMNS(*array*)

Produces the column number of the reference cell.

COS(*radians*)

Returns the cosine of the radian angle *radians*.

COUNT(*value1,value2,...*)

Counts the numbers occurring in a group of arguments.

COUNTA(*value1,value2,...*)

Counts the number of values in a group of arguments.

DATE(*year,month,day*)

Returns an integer from 1 to 65380 corresponding to a date from January 1, 1900, to December 31, 2078.

DATEVALUE(*date_text*)

Returns an integer from 1 to 65380 corresponding to a date from January 1, 1900, to December 31, 2078.

DAVERAGE(*database,field,criteria*)

Averages a *field* of *database* records satisfying the *criteria*.

DAY(*serial_number*)

Returns an integer from 1 to 31 representing a day of the month. Corresponds to a date from January 1, 1900 to December 31, 2078.

DCOUNT(*database,field,criteria*)

Counts the number of cells in a field of database records that contain numbers that satisfy the criteria.

DCOUNTA(*database,field,criteria*)

Counts number of cells in *field* of *database* records that are nonblank and satisfy the *criteria*. If you do not specify field, Excel counts all blank cells.

DDB(*cost,salvage,life,period*)

Calculates depreciation of an asset for a period of time based on initial cost, salvage value, and useful life.

DMAX(*database,field,criteria*)

Finds largest number in a *field* of *database* records that satisfies the *criteria*.

DMIN(*database,field,criteria*)

Finds smallest number in a *field* of *database* records that satisfies the *criteria*.

DOLLAR(*number,decimals*)

Rounds the number to the specified *number* of *decimals* to the right of the decimal point and converts the number to a textual currency format.

DPRODUCT(*database,field,criteria*)

Calculates product of the numbers in a *field* of *database* records that satisfy the *criteria*.

DSTDEV(*database,field,criteria*)

Approximates standard deviation based on a sample, using *database* records that satisfy the criteria.

DSTDEVP(*database,field,criteria*)

Calculates standard deviation based on entire population, using *database* records that satisfy the *criteria*.

DSUM(*database,field,criteria*)

Totals the numbers in a field of *database* records that satisfy the *criteria*.

DVAR(*database,field,criteria*)

Calculates variance of a population based on a sample, using a *field* of *database* records that satisfy the *criteria*.

DVARP(*database,field,criteria*)

Calculates variance of a population based on the entire population, using a field of *database* records that satisfy the *criteria*.

EXACT(*text1,text2*)

Returns TRUE if the two specified *text* strings are identical, otherwise FALSE.

EXP(*number*)

Returns e (2.71828182845904) raised to the power of a specified *number*.

FACT(*number*)

Returns a factorial of a specified *number*.

FALSE()

Returns the logical value FALSE.

FIND(*find_text,within_text,start_at_num*)

Produces integer position at which a *text* substring occurs in a *text* string. Search begins at 1 or at optionally specified number position. Case sensitive and cannot be used with wildcards.

FIXED(*number,decimals*)

Rounds to a specified *number* of *decimal* places and formats with a period and commas.

FV(*rate,nper,pmt,pv,type*)

Calculates the future value of an investment based on the total number of constant, periodic payments, the cost of a payment, and optionally the present value of the payments due and the type of payment arrangement .

GROWTH(*known_y's,known_x's,new_x's*)

Calculates *y*-values along an exponential curve for an array of new x-values, based on known y -and x-values.

HLOOKUP(*lookup_value,table_array,row_index_num*)

Looks across the top row of the range specified by *table_array* until a match for *lookup_value* is found (if none, the largest value less than *lookup_value* is used); then moves down that column to the row specified by *row_index_num*.

HOUR(*serial_number*)

Returns an integer from 0 to 23 representing an hour of the day. Corresponds to a time from 12:00 a.m. to 11:00 p.m. entered in Excel *serial_number* or *time_text* format.

IF(*logical_test,value_if_true,value_if_false*)

> Returns the *value_is_true* if *logical_text* is TRUE. Otherwise, *value_is_false* returns.

INDEX(*ref,row_num,column_num,area_num*)

> Produces the contents of a cell or cells specified by a reference to one or more ranges, the row and column number(s), and optionally the particular range you want.

INDEX(*array,row_num,column_num*)

> Produces the value of an element in an *array* specified by the *array*, and the element's *row* and *column number*.

INDIRECT(*ref_text,type_of_ref*)

> Returns the cell contents pointed at by the contents of another cell.

INT(*number*)

> Returns the integer resulting from rounding a *number*.

IPMT(*rate,per,nper,pv,fv,type*)

> Calculates an interest payment based on a constant interest rate, the payment period, the total number of constant, periodic payments, and the present value of the payments due. Optionally calculates the future value of the investment and the type of payment arrangement.

IRR(*values,guess*)

> Calculates an internal rate of return for a series of periodic cash flows). If you do not include a *guess*, Excel assumes 10 percent.

ISBLANK(*value*)

> Returns TRUE if argument refers to an empty cell; otherwise FALSE.

ISERR(*value*)

> Returns TRUE if argument is an Excel error *value* except #N/A (no value available); otherwise FALSE.

ISERROR(*value*)

> Returns TRUE if argument is an Excel error *value*; otherwise FALSE.

ISLOGICAL(*value*)

Returns TRUE if argument is a logical value; otherwise FALSE.

ISNA(*value*)

Returns TRUE if argument is the error value #N/A (no value available); otherwise FALSE.

ISNONTEXT(*value*)

Returns TRUE if argument is not text; otherwise FALSE.

ISNUMBER(*value*)

Returns TRUE if argument is a number; otherwise FALSE.

ISREF(*value*)

Returns TRUE if argument is a reference; otherwise FALSE.

ISTEXT(*value*)

Returns TRUE if argument is text; otherwise FALSE.

LEFT(*text,number_of_characters*)

Returns the leftmost character(s) in a *text* string specified by *num*.

LEN(*text*)

Returns the length of *text*.

LINEST(*known_y's,known_x's*)

Calculates an array representing a straight line based on array of *known_y's* and, optionally, *known_x's*.

LN(*number*)

Calculates the natural logarithm of a positive *number*.

LOG(*number,base*)

Calculates the logarithm of a positive *number* in a specified *base*. Excel assumes base 10.

LOG10(*number*)

Calculates the logarithm of a positive *number* in base 10.

LOGEST(*known_y's,known_x's*)

Calculates a horizontal array representing an exponential curve based on array of *known_y's* and, optionally, *known_x's*.

LOOKUP(*lookup_value,lookup_vector,result_vector*)

Searches the row or column array specified by *lookup_vector* until a match for *lookup_value* is found (if none is found, the largest value less than *lookup_value* is used), and then moves to the corresponding position in *result_vector*.

LOOKUP(*lookup_value,array*)

Searches an array's first column (if the array has more rows than columns) or first row (if the *array* has more columns than rows, or the same number of columns and rows) for a match to *lookup_value* (if none is found, the largest value less than *lookup_value* is used), then moves down or across to the last cell.

LOWER(*text*)

Converts text to lowercase.

MATCH(*lookup_value,lookup_array,type_of_match*)

Returns value in an array. Selection is based on the following *type_of_match* codes: if code is omitted or 1, returns largest value less than or equal to *lookup_value*. If code is 0, returns first value equal to *lookup_value*. If code is -1, returns smallest value greater than or equal to *lookup_value*.

MAX(*number1,number2,...*)

Finds the largest *number* among arguments that can contain up to 14 values.

MDETERM(*array*)

Returns a number representing the matrix determinant of a square, numeric *array*.

MID(*text,start_number,number_of_characters*)

Returns a substring of specified *text*, beginning at specified position number and continuing for specified number of characters.

MIN(*number1,number2,...*)

Finds the smallest *number* in list of up to 14 values.

MINUTE(*serial_number*)

Returns integer from 0 to 59 representing a minute of an hour entered in Excel *serial_number* or *time_text* format.

MINVERSE(*array*)

Calculates an *array* that is the inverse matrix of a square, numeric array.

MIRR(*values,finance_rate,reinvest_rate*)

Calculates a modified internal rate of return for a series of periodic cash flows.

MMULT(*array1,array2*)

Calculates the matrix product of *array1* times *array2*. Both arrays must contain only numbers, and number of columns must equal number of rows.

MOD(*number,divisor_number*)

Returns the integer remainder resulting from *number* divided by *divisor_number*.

MONTH(*serial_number*)

Returns an integer from 1 to 12 representing a month of the year.

N(*value*)

If a *value* is a number, returns that number. If *value* is logical TRUE, returns 1. If *value* is anything else, returns 0.

NA()

Returns the error value #N/A (no value is available).

NOT(*logical*)

If *logical* is FALSE, returns TRUE. If logical is TRUE, returns FALSE.

NOW()

Returns a *serial_number* corresponding to the current date and time in the PC's clock.

NPER(*rate,pmt,pv,fv,type*)

Calculates the number of periods for an investment based on constant, periodic payments, a constant interest rate, and the present value of the coming payments. Optionally calculates the future value and the type of payment arrangement.

NPV(*rate,value1,value2,…*)

Calculates the net present value of an investment based on periodic cash flows.

OR(*logical1,logical2,…*)

If all arguments in the list are FALSE, returns FALSE, otherwise returns TRUE.

PI()

Returns 3.14159265358979.

PMT(*rate,nper,pv,fv,type*)

Calculates the cost of a single payment for an investment based on a constant interest *rate*, the total number of constant, periodic payments, and the present value of the coming payments. Optionally calculates the future value of the payments and the type of payment arrangement.

PPMT(*rate,per,nper,pv,fv,type*)

Calculates payment on the principal for a specified period based on a constant interest *rate*, the total number of constant, periodic payments and the present value of the coming payments; and optionally the future value and the type of payment arrangement.

PRODUCT(*number1,number2,…*)

Calculates product from list of one to 14 values).

PROPER(*text*)

Capitalizes first letter and all letters following non-letter characters. All other letters appear lowercase.

PV(*rate,nper,pmt,fv,type*)

Calculates present value of an investment based on a constant *rate*, the total number of constant, periodic payments and the cost of a single payment. Optionally calculates the future value of the coming payments and the type of payment arrangement.

RAND()

Returns random number between 0 and 1, including 0 but not 1. Regenerates each time Excel calculates the cell.

RATE(*nper,pmt,pv,fv,type,guess*)

Calculates interest rate per period based on the total number of constant, periodic payments, the cost of a single payment, and the present value of the coming payments. Optionally calculates the future value, the *type* of payment arrangement, and your *guess* of the rate to ensure RATE iterations converge. If you do not specify a guess, Excel assumes 10 percent.

REPLACE(*old_text,start_num,num_chars,new_text*)

Replaces a text's substring with a new substring, starting at a specified position and with a specified length.

REPT(*text,number_times*)

Repeats a *text* string a specified number of times.

RIGHT(*text,number_of_chars*)

Returns the *text* of a specified number of characters of a text string. If you do not include *number_of_chars*, Excel assumes 1.

ROUND(*number,number_of_digits*)

Rounds *number* to a specified *number_of_digits*.

ROW(*reference*)

Returns row number(s) of a specified row or range of rows. If you do not specify a row, Excel returns the row in which the function appears.

ROWS(*array*)

Returns the number of rows in a specified *array*.

SEARCH(*find_text,within_text,start_at_num*)

Produces the integer position at which a *text* substring occurs in a text string. Same as FIND, except SEARCH allows wildcards and is not case sensitive.

SECOND(*serial_number*)

Returns an integer from 1 to 31 representing a day of the month. Corresponds to a date from January 1, 1900, to December 31, 2078, entered in Excel *serial_number* or *date_text* formats.

SIGN(*number*)

Returns 1 if specified *number* is positive, 0 if 0, -1 if negative.

SIN(*radians*)

Returns sine of the specified *number* of radians in an angle.

SLN(*cost,salvage,life*)

Calculates the straight-line depreciation for an asset for a single period.

SQRT(*number*)

Calculates the positive square root of a *number*.

STDEV(*number1,number2,...*)

Calculates the standard deviation of a population with up to 14 arguments. Calculations use the "non-biased" method.

STDEVP(*number1,number2,...*)

Calculates the standard deviation of a population with up to 14 arguments. Calculations use the "biased" method.

SUBSTITUTE(*text,old_text,new_text,instance_number*)

Substitutes one substring for another substring. Optionally you can specify the number of times the substring is replaced.

SUM(*number1,number2,...*)

Sums up to 14 *numbers* . Arguments can contain empty cells, logical values, and numbers in text format.

SYD(*cost,salvage,life,per*)

Calculates the sum-of-years' digits depreciation for an asset for a specified period, based on the initial *cost*, *salvage* value, useful *life*, and *period* of the asset.

T(*value*)

If a *value* is text or a cell address containing text, returns the text. Otherwise returns "" (null text).

TAN(*radians*)

Returns the tangent of the angle defined by specified number of *radians*.

TEXT(*value,format_text*)

Converts the *value* to specified text format.

TIME(*hour,minute,second*)

Returns a *serial_number* (decimal fraction from 0 through .9999) corresponding to the time specified in *hour,minute,second* format.

TIMEVALUE(*time_text*)

Returns a *serial_number* (decimal fraction from 0 through .9999) corresponding to the time specified in *time_text* format.

TRANSPOSE(*array*)

Transposes contents of an array's rows and columns.

TREND(*known_y's,known_x's,new_x's*)

Calculates y-values along a straight line for an array of new x-values, based on known y- and x-values.

TRIM(*text*)

Removes all spaces from a *text* string except for a single space between words.

TRUE()

Returns the logical value TRUE.

TRUNC(*number*)

Truncates a *number* past the decimal point.

TYPE(*value*)

Returns number representing the data type of a *value*, specifically, 1 = number, 2 = text, 4 = logical value, 16 = error value, and 64 = array.

UPPER(*text*)

Converts *text* to uppercase.

VALUE(*text*)

Converts *text* in Excel to a constant number, date or time format.

VAR(*number1,number2,...*)

Calculates the variance of a population based on a sample of up to 14 arguments.

VARP(*number1,number2,...*)

Calculates the variance of a population based on the population, represented by up to 14 arguments.

VLOOKUP(*lookup_value,table_array,col_index*)

Returns the contents of a cell, which Excel locates by looking down the leftmost column of the range specified by *table_array* until it finds a match for *lookup_value*. If no match is found, uses the largest value less than *lookup_value,* and moves across that row to the column specified by *col_index*.

WEEKDAY(*serial_number*)

Returns an integer from 1 to 7 representing a day of the week. Corresponds to days Sunday to Saturday entered in Excel *serial_number* or *date_text* format.

YEAR(*serial_number*)

Returns an integer from 1900 to 2078 representing a year you enter in Excel *serial_number* or *date_text* format.

MACRO FUNCTIONS

This section lists alphabetically and briefly describes all Excel macro functions with the exception of macros that duplicate worksheet functions.

Macro functions take and pass back data through variables called *arguments*. Each macro function has its own list of arguments, which are enclosed in parentheses and directly follow the function name. In this book, if an argument is printed normally, it is mandatory. If it is *italicized*, it is optional. If it is followed by an ellipsis (...), it is part of a repeatable series. Macro functions can have up to 13 arguments. You can use macro functions by themselves or with each other to customize Excel in sophisticated ways.

A1.R1C1(*r1c1*)

Duplicates selecting Options Workspace R1C1

ABSREF(*ref_text,ref*)

Returns a new absolute cell reference or range resulting from the combination of the absolute reference *ref* with the relative reference (in R1C1 format) *ref_text*.

ACTIVATE(*window_text,pane_num*)

Duplicates pressing F6, activating a pane in a window.

ACTIVATE.NEXT()

Duplicates pressing Ctrl+F6, activating next window.

ACTIVATE.PREV()

Duplicates pressing Shift+Ctrl+F6, activating preceding window.

ACTIVE.CELL()

Returns the active cell reference in external reference format. Generally yields the value in the active cell.

ADD.ARROW()

Duplicates the Chart Add ARrow command.

ADD.BAR()

Creates a blank menu bar and returns bar ID number.

ADD.COMMAND(*bar_num,menu_pos,menu_ref*)

Adds one or more commands to a menu bar.

ADD.MENU(*bar_num,menu_ref*)

Adds a menu to a menu bar (appends to right of bar if there are preceding menus) and returns position number.

ADD.OVERLAY()

Duplicates the Chart Add Overlay command.

ALERT(*message_text,type_num*)

> Shows a message you specify in a dialog box and waits for button selection..

ALIGNMENT(*type_number*)
ALIGNMENT?(*type_number*)

> Duplicates the FormaT Alignment command.

APP.ACTIVATE(*title_text,wait_log*)

> Activates an application with a title bar you specify by *title_text* (if you do not specify *title_text* , the Excel program runs) either immediately (if *wait_log* is FALSE) or directly after Excel activates (if you omit *wait_log* or it is TRUE).

APP.MAXIMIZE()

> Duplicates Control MaXimize for application window.

APP.MINIMIZE()

> Duplicates Control MiNimize for application window.

APP.MOVE(*x_num,y_num*)
APP.MOVE?(*x_num,y_num*)

> Duplicates Control Move for application window.

APP.RESTORE()

> Duplicates Control Restore for application window.

APP.SIZE(*x_num,y_num*)
APP.SIZE?(*x_num,y_num*)

> Duplicates Control Size for application window.

APPLY.NAMES(*name_array,ignore,use_rowcol,omit_col, omit_row,name_order,append*)
APPLY.NAMES?(*name_array,ignore,use_rowcol,omit_col, omit_row,name_order,append*)

> Duplicates the FoRmula Apply Names command.

ARGUMENT(*name_text,data_type_num*)
ARGUMENT?(*name_text,data_type_num,ref*)

> Describes arguments to use in a function macro by name, type, and location. Function macros can take as many as 13 arguments.

ARRANGE.ALL()

Duplicates the Window Arrange All command.

ATTACH.TEXT(*attach_to_num,series_num,point_num*)
ATTACH.TEXT?(*attach_to_num,series_num,point_num*)

Duplicates the Chart Attach Text command.

AXES(*main_cat,main_value,over_cat,over_value*)
AXES?(*main_cat,main_value,over_cat,over_value*)

Duplicates the Chart AXes command.

BEEP(*number*)

Beeps the computer with a tone specified by numbers 1 through 4. If you omit an argument, Excel assumes 1. This effect varies with different types of computers. For example, on the IBM PC, all four tones generate the same sound.

BORDER(*outline,left,right,top,bottom,shade*)
BORDER?(*outline,left,right,top,bottom,shade*)

Duplicates the FormaT Border command.

BREAK()

Breaks macro execution out of a FOR-NEXT or WHILE-NEXT loop to proceed to next instruction.

CALCULATE.DOCUMENT()

Duplicates Options Calculate Document (shifted command). Calculates the active document.

CALCULATE.NOW()

Duplicates Options Calculate Now and Chart Calculate Now for all open documents.

CALCULATION(*type_num,iter,max_num,max_change, update,precision,date_1904*)
CALCULATION?(*type_num,iter,max_num,max_change, update,precision,date_1904*)

Duplicates the Options Calculation command.

CALL(*call_text,argument1,...*)

Calls a procedure from a Microsoft Windows dynamic library. For advanced programmers only.

CALLER()

Returns the reference of the cell containing the function that started the currrently running function macro.

CANCEL.COPY()

Duplicates **Esc** to eliminate the marquee surrounding a cut or copied area.

CANCEL.KEY(*enable,macro_ref*)

If you omit *enable* or if *enable* is FALSE, disables **Esc** from interrupting the current macro. If *enable* is TRUE and you omit *macro_ref*, enables **Esc** to interrupt again. If *enable* is TRUE and you specify *macro_ref*, sets **Esc** to transfer execution to *macro_ref*.

CELL.PROTECTION(*locked,hidden*)
CELL.PROTECTION?(*locked,hidden*)

Duplicates the Forma**T** Cell **P**rotection command.

CHANGE.LINK(*old_line,new_link*)
CHANGE.LINK?(*old_line,new_link*)

Duplicates selecting **F**ile **L**inks and a document, then selecting the Change button and typing the name of another document. The two arguments must be the names of linked files enclosed in quotation marks.

CHECK.COMMAND(*bar_num,menu_pos,*
command_pos,check)

Adds or removes a check mark next to a *command* in a menu bar.

CLEAR(*number*)

CLEAR?(*number*)

Duplicates the **E**dit Cl**E**ar command.

CLOSE(*save_logical*)

Duplicates Control **C**lose for active document window.

CLOSE.ALL()

Duplicates **F**ile **C**lose All (shifted command).

COLUMN.WIDTH(*width_num,ref*)
COLUMN.WIDTH?(*width_num,ref*)

Duplicates the FormaT Column Width command.

COMBINATION(*number*)
COMBINATION?(number)

Duplicates the Gallery ComBination command.

COPY()

Duplicates the Edit Copy command.

COPY.CHART(*number*)
COPY.CHART?(*number*)

Included for compatibility with Macintosh Excel.

COPY.PICTURE(*appearance,size*)

Duplicates Edit Copy Picture (shifted command).

CREATE.NAMES(*top,left,bottom,right*)
CREATE.NAMES?(*top,left,bottom,right*)

Duplicates the FoRmula Create Names command.

CUT()

Duplicates the Edit CuT command.

DATA.DELETE()
DATA.DELETE?()

Duplicates the Data Delete command.

DATA.FIND(*logical*)

Duplicates the Data Find command.

DATA.FIND.NEXT()

Duplicates the Data Find command. Pressing the down-arrow key finds the next matching record in a database).

DATA.FIND.PREV()

Duplicates the Data Find command. Pressing the up-arrow finds the preceding matching record in a database.

DATA.FORM()

Duplicates the Data FOrm command.

DATA.SERIES(*row_col,type,date,step,stop*)
DATA.SERIES?(*row_col,type,date,step,stop*)

Duplicates the Data SeRies command.

DEFINE.NAME(*name_text,refers_to,macro_type,shortcut_text*)
DEFINE.NAME?(*name_text,refers_to,macro_type,shortcut_text*)

Duplicates the FoRmula Define Name command.

DELETE.ARROW()

Duplicates the Chart Delete ARrow command.

DELETE.BAR(*bar_num*)

Deletes a custom menu bar.

DELETE.COMMAND(*bar_num,menu_pos,command_pos*)

Deletes a command from a menu bar.

DELETE.FORMAT(*format_text*)

Duplicates the FormaT Number command to delete a specified format.

DELETE.MENU(*bar_num,menu_pos*)

Deletes a menu on a menu bar.

DELETE.NAME(*name_text*)

Duplicates the FoRmula Define Name command to delete a specified *name*.

DELETE.OVERLAY()

Duplicates the Chart Delete Overlay command.

DEREF(*reference*)

Returns the value(s) in the cells you reference.

DIALOG.BOX(*dialog_ref*)

Brings up a dialog box based on specifications in area *dialog_ref* of a worksheet or macro sheet. Directs saving of values you enter in dialog box and returns the item number of the button you press.

DIRECTORY(*path_text*)

Changes drive and directory to the path name specified by *path_text* and returns the new directory in text format. If you omit *path_text*, returns current directory.

DISABLE.INPUT(*logical*)

If argument is TRUE, disables input from the keyboard and mouse. Otherwise, enables input.

DISPLAY(*formula,gridline,heading,zero,color*)

Duplicates the Options Display command.

DISPLAY(*cell,formula,value,format,protect,names, precedents,dependents,note*)

Duplicates commands from the Info menu.

DOCUMENTS()

Returns an array of text names of all open documents in alphabetical order.

ECHO(*logical*)

If argument is FALSE, turns off screen updating while macro is running. If TRUE or you omit *logical*, resumes screen updating.

EDIT.DELETE(*num*)
EDIT.DELETE?(*num*)

Duplicates the Edit Delete command.

ENABLE.COMMAND(*bar_num,menu_pos, command_pos, enable*)

If *enable* is TRUE, enables specified command in a menu bar. Otherwise disables it.

ERROR(*enable,macro_ref*)

Specifies error handling during macro execution. If *enable* is FALSE, all error checking turns off. If *enable* is TRUE and you omit *macro_ref*, standard error checking turns on. If *enable* is TRUE and you include *macro_ref*, an error causes execution to transfer to the specified macro.

EXEC(*program_text,window_number*)

Runs program you specify in separate window under Microsoft Windows (requires version 2.0 or higher) and returns the Windows task ID number for the program.

EXECUTE(*channel_num,execute_text*)

Use with the INITIATE macro function. Executes specified commands in the application connected to the specified channel. Requires Microsoft Windows 2.0 or higher.

EXTRACT(*unique_log*)
EXTRACT?(*unique_log*)

Duplicates the Data Extract command.

FCLOSE(*file_number*)

Closes the file you specify, which must have been opened with FOPEN.

FILE.CLOSE(*save_logical*)

Duplicates the File Close command.

FILE.DELETE(*name_text*)
FILE.DELETE?(*name_text*)

Duplicates the File Delete command.

FILES(*directory.text*)

Returns a horizontal array of the file names in the specified directory.

FILL.DOWN()

Duplicates the Edit Fill Down command.

FILL.LEFT()

Duplicates Edit Fill Left (H) (shifted command).

FILL.RIGHT()

Duplicates the Edit Fill Right command.

FILL.UP()

Duplicates Edit Fill Up (W) (shifted command).

FONT(*name,size*)
FONT?(*name,size*)

Included for compatibility with Macintosh Excel.

FOPEN(*file_text,access_number*)

Opens an existing *file* for read/write access (*access_number*=1), read-only access

(*access_number*=2), or creates a new file
(*access_number*=3), then returns document ID number.

FOR(*counter_name*,*start_num*,*end_num*,*step_num*)

Executes all instructions between the macro and a
NEXT statement in a loop until *counter_name* exceeds
end_num.

FORMAT.FONT(*name_text*,*size_num*,*bold*,*italic*, *underline*,*strike*)
FORMAT.FONT?(*name_text*,*size_num*,*bold*,*italic*, *underline*,*strike*)

Duplicates the Format Font command for a worksheet or
macro sheet.

FORMAT.FONT(*color*,*backgd*,*apply*,*name*, *name_text*, *size*,*bold*,*italic*,*underline*,*strike*)
FORMAT.FONT?(*color*,*backgd*,*apply*,*name*,*name_text*, *size*,*bold*,*italic*,.MDUL/underline.MDNM/,.MDUL/ strike.MDNM/)

Duplicates the Format Font command for a chart.

FORMAT.LEGEND(*position_num*)
FORMAT.LEGEND?(*position_num*)

Duplicates the Format Legend command.

FORMAT.MOVE(*x_pos*,*y_pos*)
FORMAT.MOVE?(*x_pos*,*y_pos*)

Duplicates the Format Move command.

FORMAT.NUMBER(*format_text*)
FORMAT.NUMBER?(*format_text*)

Duplicates the Format Number command.

FORMAT.SIZE(*width*,*height*)
FORMAT.SIZE?(**width**,**height**)

Duplicates the Format Size command.

FORMAT.TEXT(*x_align*,*y_align*,*vert_text*,*auto_text*, *auto_size*,*show_key*.MDNM/,.MDUL/*show_value*.MDNM/)
FORMAT.TEXT?(.MDUL/*x_align*.MDNM/,.MDUL/

y_align.MDNM/,.MDUL/*vert_text*.MDNM/,.MDUL/
auto_text.MDNM/,.MDUL/*auto_size*.MDNM/,.MDUL/
show_key.MDNM/,.MDUL/*show_value*.MDNM/)

>   Duplicates the Format Text command.

FORMULA(*formula_text,ref*)

>   If the active document is a worksheet, duplicates
>   entering a formula in a cell (if you omit *ref*, Excel uses
>   the active cell). If the active document is a chart,
>   duplicates entering text labels or SERIES functions.

FORMULA.ARRAY(*formula_text,ref*)

>   Duplicates pressing **Ctrl+Shift+Enter** to enter an array
>   *formula*. If you omit *ref*, Excel uses the current
>   selection.

FORMULA.FILL(*formula_text,ref*)

>   Duplicates pressing **Shift** to enter a *formula*. If you omit
>   *ref*, Excel uses the current selection.

FORMULA.FIND(*text,in_num,at_num,by_num,direction*)
FORMULA.FIND?(*text,in_num,at_num,by_num,direction*)
>   Duplicates the FoRmula Find command.

FORMULA.FIND.NEXT()
FORMULA.FIND.PREV()

>   Duplicates pressing **F7** and **Shift+F7**, respectively.
>   Finds next and previous occurrences of the value in the
>   Formula Find dialog box.

FORMULA.GOTO(*reference*)
FORMULA.GOTO?(*reference*)

>   Duplicates the Formula Goto command or pressing **F5**

FORMULA.REPLACE(*find_text,replace_text,look_at,*
look_by,current_cell.MDNM/)
FORMULA.REPLACE?(.MDUL/*find_text*.MDNM/
,.MDUL/*replace_text*.MDNM/,.MDUL/*look_at*.MDNM/
,.MDUL/*look_by*.MDNM/,.MDUL/*current_cell*.MDNM/)
>   Duplicates the Formula REplace.

FPOS(*file_number,position_number*)

>   Sets starting position for reading from or writing to
>   specified file (which you must have opened with

FOPEN). If you do not specify *position_number*, Excel returns current position.

FREAD(*file_number,num_chars*)

Starting from current position in specified file (which you must have opened with FOPEN), returns specified number of characters.

FREADLN(*file_number*)

Starting from current position in specified file (which you must have opened with FOPEN), returns all characters until the end of the line (marked by carriage return and/or linefeed).

FREEZE.PANES(*logical*)

Duplicates the Options Freeze Panes command if argument is TRUE. Otherwise duplicates the Options Unfreeze Panes command.

FSIZE(*file_number*)

Returns the number of characters in the specified file (which you must open with FOPEN).

FULL(*logical*)

If argument is TRUE, duplicates selecting Control Maximize for the active document window. If FALSE, duplicates selecting Control R.MDNM/Restore to restore window to preceding size.

FWRITE(*file_number,text*)

Starting from current position in specified file (which you must have opened with FOPEN), writes specified text to the file.

FWRITELN(*file_number,text*)

Starting from current position in specified file (which you must have opened with FOPEN), writes specified text and carriage return/linefeed.

GALLERY.AREA(*number,*.MDUL/*delete_overlay*.MDNM/)
GALLERY.AREA?(.MDUL/*number*.MDNM/,, .MDUL/*delete_overlay*.MDNM/)

Duplicates the Gallery Area command.

GALLERY.BAR(*number,delete_overlay*)
GALLERY.BAR?(*number,delete_overlay*)
   Duplicates the Gallery Bar command.

GALLERY.COLUMN(*number,delete_overlay*)
GALLERY.COLUMN?(*number,delete_overlay*)
   Duplicates the Gallery Column command.

GALLERY.LINE(*number,delete_overlay*)
GALLERY.LINE?(*number,delete_overlay*)
   Duplicates the Gallery Line command.

GALLERY.PIE(*number,delete_overlay*)
GALLERY.PIE?(*number,delete_overlay*)
   Duplicates the Gallery Pie command.

GALLERY.SCATTER(*number,delete_overlay*)
GALLERY.SCATTER?(*number,delete_overlay*)
   Duplicates the Gallery Scatter command.

GET.BAR()
   Returns the ID number of the active menu bar.

GET.CELL(*type_of_info,reference*)
   Returns a wide variety of information about the
   contents, formatting, and location of the first cell in
   reference (if you omit *reference*, Excel uses the current
   selection). Twenty-three *type_of_info* codes exist,
   numbered 1-23.

GET.CHART.ITEM(*x_y_index,point_index,item_text*)
   Returns the horizontal or vertical position of a point on a
   chart item.

**GET.DEF(.MDUL/*def_text*.MDNM/.MDUL/
.MDNM/,.MDUL/*document*.MDNM/)**
   Returns the range name for specified reference in
   specified document.

GET.DOCUMENT(*type_of_info,name_text*)
   Returns wide variety of information about the specified
   document (if you omit *name_text*, Excel uses the active

document). Twenty-six *type_of_info* codes exist, numbered 1-26.

GET.FORMULA(*reference*)

Returns the contents of the first cell in *reference*, in text format.

GET.NAME(*name_text*)

Returns the definition of the specified range. Equivalent of the Refers To text box for Formula Define Name.

GET.NOTE(*cell_ref,start_char,count_char*)

Returns substring of note attached to *cell_ref*. If you omit *start_char*, Excel assumes 1. If you omit *count_chart*, Excel assumes length of entire note.

GET.WINDOW(*type_of_info,name_text*)

Returns wide variety of information about the specified window (if you omit *name_text*, Excel uses the active window). Sixteen *type_of_info* codes exist, numbered 1-16.

GET.WORKSPACE(*type_of_info*)

Returns wide variety of information about the workspace. Nineteen *type_of_info* codes exist, numbered 1-19.

GOTO(*reference*)

Transfers macro execution to the first cell in reference.

GRIDLINES(*cat_major,cat_minor,value_major,value_minor*)
GRIDLINES?(*cat_major,cat_minor,value_major,value_minor*)

Duplicates the Chart Gridlines command.

HALT()

Interrupts macro execution.

HELP(*help_ref*)

Shows help topic you specify. If you omit *help_ref*, duplicates the Help Index command.

HIDE()

Duplicates the Window Hide command.

HLINE(**number_cols**)

Scrolls the active window horizontally by specified number of columns. If *number_cols* is negative, scrolls left rather than right.

HPAGE(**number_windows**)

Scrolls the active window horizontally by specified number of window widths. If *number_windows* is negative, scrolls left rather than right.

HSCROLL(**scroll,col_log**)

If *col_log* is TRUE, scrolls to column *scroll*; otherwise, scrolls to the column that's *scroll* percent away from the leftmost edge of the document.

INITIATE(**app_text,topic_text**)

Opens a DDE channel to an application and returns the number of the open channel (requires Microsoft Windows 2.0 or higher).

INPUT(**prompt,type,title,default,x_pos,Y_pos**)

Shows a dialog box and returns the data you enter in the box.

INSERT(**shift_num**)
INSERT?(**shift_num**)

Duplicates the Edit Insert command.

JUSTIFY()

Duplicates the FoRmat Justify command.

LEGEND(**logical**)

Duplicates the Chart Add Legend command if argument is TRUE. Otherwise, deletes the legend.

LINKS(**doc_text**)

Returns a horizontal array of names of worksheets linked to the specified document.

LIST.NAMES()

Duplicates the FoRmula Paste Name command with the Paste List button.

MAIN.CHART(*type,stack,100,vary,overlap,drop,
hilo,overlap%,cluster,angle*)

Duplicates the FoRmat Main Chart command.

MAIN.CHART.TYPE(*type*)

Included for compatibility with Macintosh Excel.

MESSAGE(*logical,text*)

If argument is TRUE, displays specified text in the
message area of the status bar. If FALSE, removes all
messages from status bar, and returns status bar to
normal.

MOVE(*x_pos,y_pos,window_text*)

Duplicates the Control Move command.

NAMES(*doc_text*)

Returns a horizontal array of all names defined in the
specified document. If you omit *doc_text*, Excel uses the
active document.

NEW(*type_number*)
NEW?(*type_number*)

Duplicates the File New command.

NEW.WINDOW()

Duplicates the Window New Window command.

NEXT()

Defines the bottom end of a FOR-NEXT or WHILE-
NEXT loop.

NOTE(*add_text,cell_ref,start_char,count_char*)

Starting at the specified position in the note attached to a
specified cell, replaces specified number of characters
with new text.

OFFSET(*ref,rows,cols,height,width*)

Takes the cell reference or range specified by *ref* and
offsets it by a specified number of rows and columns,
then returns the resulting new reference. Optionally
makes the reference a specified number of rows high
and columns wide.

ON.DATA(*document_text,macro_text*)

Runs a specified macro when an application sends data to a particular document.

ON.KEY(*key_text,macro_text*)

Runs a specified macro when you press a certain key (or **Alt** **Ctrl** and/or **Shift** keystroke combination).

ON.TIME(*time,macro_text,tolerance,insert_log*)

Runs a specified macro at a particular time.

ON.WINDOW(*window_text,macro_text*)

Runs a specified macro when you activate a particular window.

OPEN(*file_text,update_ext,read_only_rem*)
OPEN?(*file_text,update_links,read_only*)

Duplicates the File Open command.

OPEN.LINKS(*doc_text1,doc_text2,,read_only_log*)
OPEN.LINKS?(*doc_text1,doc_text2,,read_only_log*)

Duplicates the File Links command.

OVERLAY(*type,stack,100,vary,overlap,drop,hilo,overlap%,cluster,angle,series,auto*)

Duplicates the FoRmat Overlay command.

OVERLAY.CHART.TYPE(*type*)

Included for compatibility with Macintosh Excel.

PAGE.SETUP(*head,foot,left,right,top,bot,heading,grid*)
PAGE.SETUP?(*head,foot,left,right,top,bot,heading,grid*)
PAGE.SETUP(*head,foot,left,right,top,bot,size*)
PAGE.SETUP?(*head,foot,left,right,top,bot,size*)

Duplicates the File Page SeTup command.

PARSE(parse_text)

Duplicates the Data Parse command.

PASTE()

Duplicates the Edit Paste command.

PASTE.LINK()

Duplicates the Edit Paste Link command.

PASTE.SPECIAL(*paste_what,operation,skip_blanks, transpose*)
PASTE.SPECIAL?(*paste_what,operation,skip_blanks, transpose*)

Duplicates the Edit Paste Special command for pasting into a worksheet or macro sheet.

PASTE.SPECIAL(*row_col,series,categories,apply*)
PASTE.SPECIAL?(*row_col,series,categories,apply*)

Duplicates the Edit Paste Special command for pasting from a worksheet into a chart.

PASTE.SPECIAL(*paste_what*)
PASTE.SPECIAL?(*paste_what*)

Duplicates selecting Edit Paste Special for pasting from one chart into another chart.

PATTERNS(*b_auto,b_style,b_color,b_wt,shadow,a_auto, a_pattern,a_fore,a_back,invert,*APPLY)
PATTERNS(LINE,*t_major,t_minor,t_label*)
PATTERNS(LINE)
PATTERNS(LINE,*m_auto,m_style,m_fore, m_back,*APPLY)
PATTERNS(LINE,*h_width,h_length,h_type*)

Duplicates the FormaT Patterns command.

POKE(*channel_num,item_text,data_ref*)

Sends data to an item in an application connected to the specified channel (which you must have opened by the INITIATE function). Requires Microsoft Windows 2.0 or higher.

PRECISION(*logical*)

Duplicates the Options Calculation command and setting the Precision as Displayed check box (TRUE argument turns it off, FALSE on).

PREFERRED()

Duplicates the Gallery PReferred command.

PRINT(*range,from,to,copies,draft,preview,parts*)
PRINT?(*range,from,to,copies,draft,preview,parts*)

> Duplicates the File Print command.

PRINTER.SETUP(*printer_text*)
PRINTER.SETU?P(*printer_text*)

> Duplicates the File PRinter Setup.

PROTECT.DOCUMENT(*contents,windows*)
PROTECT.DOCUMENT?(*contents,windows*)

> If a worksheet or macro sheet is the active document, duplicates selecting Options Protect Document (when either or both arguments are TRUE) and Options Unprotect Document (when both arguments are FALSE). If a chart is the active document, duplicates selecting Chart Protect Document (when either or both arguments are TRUE) and Chart Unprotect Document (when both arguments are FALSE).

QUIT()

> Duplicates the File EXit command.

REFTEXT(*ref,a1*)

> Converts a reference to an absolute reference in text format.

REGISTER(*module_text,procedure_text,argument_text*)

> Returns text value for use with the CALL function. For advanced programmers only.

RELREF(*ref,rel_to_ref*)

> Returns the relative location of *ref* with respect to the first cell of *rel_to_ref* in R1C1 format.

REMOVE.PAGE.BREAK()

> Duplicates the Options Remove Page Break command.

RENAME.COMMAND(*bar_num,menu_pos,*
command_pos,name_text)

> Replaces the name of a command on a menu with a different name.

REPLACE.FONT(*font,name_text,size_num,bold, italic,underline,strike*)

Duplicates selecting Format Font, then a font number, the Font button, a new font, and the Replace button.

REQUEST(*channel_num,item_text*)

Returns an array of data resulting from information request (specified by *item_text*) from the application connected to the specified channel (which you must open with the INITIATE function). Requires Microsoft Windows 2.0 or higher.

RESTART(*level_number*)

Removes specified number of return addresses from the stack, preventing subroutines from returning to their calling macros. If you omit *level_number*, Excel removes all return addresses.

RESULT(*type_number*)

Use with a function macro to define the data type of the return value.

RETURN(*value*)

Interrupts current macro execution and returns control to whatever initiated the macro.

ROW.HEIGHT(*height_num,ref,standard_height*)
ROW.HEIGHT?(*height_num,ref,standard_height*)

Duplicates the FoRmat Row Height command.

RUN(*reference*)
RUN?(*reference*)

Duplicates the Macro Run command.

SAVE()

Duplicates the File Save command.

SAVE.AS(*name_text,type_num,passwd_text,backup*)
SAVE.AS?(*name_text,type_num,passwd_text,backup*)

Duplicates the File Save As command.

SAVE.WORKSPACE(*name_text*)
SAVE.WORKSPACE?(*name_text*)

Duplicates the File Save Workspace command.

SCALE(*cross,cat_labels,cat_marks,between,max,reverse*)

Duplicates the FoRmat Scale command when the category axis is selected and the chart is not a scatter chart.

**SCALE(*min,max,major,minor,cross,logarithmic,*
reverse,max)**

Duplicates the FoRmat Scale command when the value axis is selected or the chart is a scatter chart.

SELECT(*selection,active_cell*)

Selects cells or changes the active cell. For worksheets and macro sheets only.

SELECT(*item_text*)

Selects a chart object based on one of 23 *item_text* codes. For charts only.

SELECT.CHART()

Included for compatibility with Macintosh Excel.

SELECT.END(*direction_num*)

Duplicates pressing Ctrl+Arrow Key. Moves active cell to the next block edge in specified direction (1=Left, 2=Right, 3=Up, 4=Down).

SELECT.LAST.CELL()

Selects the lowest and rightmost cell containing a value, format, or formula, or is referred to by a formula.

SELECT.PLOT.AREA()

Included for compatibility with Macintosh Excel.

SELECT.SPECIAL(*type_number,value_types,levels*)

Duplicates the FoRmula Select Special command.

SELECTION()

Returns the reference of the current selection as an external reference. Generally yields the value in the selection.

SEND.KEYS(*key_text,wait_log*)

Sends specified keystrokes to the active Microsoft Windows (version 2.0 or higher) application, granting control of programs other than Excel.

SET.CRITERIA()

Duplicates the Data Set Criteria command.

SET.DATABASE()

Duplicates the Data Set DataBase command.

SET.NAME(*name_text,value*)

Assigns specified *value* to a variable name on the macro sheet for temporary storage during macro execution. If you omit the *value* argument, Excel deletes *name_text*.

SET.PAGE.BREAK()

Duplicates the Options Set Page Break command.

SET.PREFERRED()

Duplicates the Gallery SeT Preferred command.

SET.PRINT.AREA()

Duplicates the Options Set Print Area command.

SET.PRINT.TITLES()

Duplicates the Options Set Print Titles command.

SET.VALUE(*ref,values*)

Sets values of specified cells.

SHORT.MENUS(*logical*)

If a worksheet or macro sheet is the active document, duplicates the Options Short Menus command (when argument is TRUE) and Options Full Menus (when argument is FALSE). If a chart is the active document, duplicates selecting Chart Short Menus (when argument is TRUE) and Chart Full Menus (when argument is FALSE).

SHOW.ACTIVE.CELL()

Duplicates Ctrl+Backspace. Brings the active cell into view in the current window.

SHOW.BAR(*bar_num*)

Shows the specified menu bar. If you omit *bar_num*, Excel displays the standard menu bar(s) appropriate for the active window.

SHOW.CLIPBOARD().

Included for compatibility with Macintosh Excel.

SHOW.INFO(*enable_log*)

Duplicates the Window Show Info command (if *enable_log* is TRUE, activates the Info window) and Window Show Document (if Info window is active and *enable_log* if FALSE, activates the document for that Info window).

SIZE(*width,height,windox_text*)

Duplicates Control SiZe for document window.

SORT(*sort_by,key1,order1,key2,order2,key3,order3*)
SORT?(*sort_by,key1,order1,key2,order2,key3,order3*)

Duplicates the Data Sort command.

SPLIT(*col_split,row_split*)

Duplicates the Control Split command for document window.

STEP()

Initiates single-stepping macro execution. Useful for debugging.

STYLE(*bold,italic*)
STYLE?(.MDUL/*bold*.MDNM/,.MDUL/*italic*.MDNM/)

Included for compatibility with Macintosh Excel.

Subroutines: *ref(arg1,arg2)*

A subroutine is a macro called by another macro (main macro) to perform small tasks. When a subroutine completes execution, it returns control to the main macro. Subroutines are identified by a reference directly followed by parentheses that optionally contain arguments. When Excel encounters subroutines, the main macro temporarily transfers control to the first cell in the reference. The subroutine then executes until it runs out of instructions or encounters a RETURN instruction.

TABLE(*row_ref,column_ref*)
TABLE?(*row_ref,column_ref*)

Duplicates the Data Table command.

TERMINATE(*channel_num*)

Closes the specified channel, which you must have opened with the INITIATE function (requires Microsoft Windows 2.0 or higher).

TEXTREF(*text,a1*)

Converts text into a reference.

UNDO()

Duplicates the Edit Undo command.

UNHIDE(*window_text*)

Duplicates the Window Unhide command.

UNLOCKED.NEXT()
UNLOCKED.PREV()

Duplicates pressing **Tab** or **Shift+Tab**, respectively, to move the active cell to the next or preceding unlocked cell in a worksheet you protect.

VLINE(*number_rows*)

Scrolls the active window vertically by specified number of rows. If *number_rows* is negative, scrolls up rather than down.

VPAGE(*number_windows*)

Scrolls the active window vertically by specified number of windows. If *number_windows* is negative, scrolls up rather than down.

VSCROLL(*scroll,row_log*)

If *row_log* is TRUE, scrolls to row *scroll*; otherwise, scrolls to the row that is *scroll* percent away from the top of the window.

WAIT(*serial_number*)

Pauses a macro until the time specified by
serial_number.

WHILE(*logical_test*)

Executes all instructions between it and a NEXT
statement in a loop until the argument is FALSE.

WINDOWS()

Returns a horizontal text array of the names of all
windows on the screen.

WORKSPACE(*fixed,decimals,r1c1,scroll,status, formula,menu,remote*)
WORKSPACE?(.MDUL/*fixed*.MDNM/,.MDUL/
decimals.MDNM/,.MDUL/*r1c1*.MDNM/,.MDUL/
scroll.MDNM/,.MDUL/.MDUL/*status*.MDNM/,.MDUL/
formula.MDNM/,.MDUL/*menu*.MDNM/,.MDUL/
remote.MDNM/)

Duplicates the Options Workspace command.

MACRO KEY CODES

To represent most characters in a macro, you type the
character represented on the screen. However, some
keyboard keys do not display a character when the key is
pressed. For these, use the following codes:

Key	*Code*
Backspace	{BACKSPACE} or {BS}
Break	{BREAK}
Caps Lock	{CAPSLOCK}
Clear	{CLEAR}
Del	{DELETE} or {DEL}
Down	{DOWN}
End	{END}
Enter	{ENTER} or ~ (tilde)
Esc	{ESCAPE} or {ESC}

Help	{HELP}
Home	{HOME}
Ins	{INSERT}
Left	{LEFT}
Num Lock	{NUMLOCK}
PgDn	{PGDN}
PgUp	{PGUP}
Prtsc	{PRTSC}
Right	{RIGHT}
Tab	{TAB}
Up	{UP}
F1	{F1}
F2	{F2}
F3	{F3}
F4	{F4}
F5	{F5}
F6	{F6}
F7	{F7}
F8	{F8}
F9	{F9}
F10	{F10}
F11	{F11}
F12	{F12}
F13	{F13}
F14	{F14}
F15	{F15}
F16	{F16}

You also can specify keys to combine with other keys. To combine with **Shift**, use a plus sign (+). To combine with **Ctrl**, use a caret (^). To combine with **Alt**, use a percent sign (%).

Index